Discovering the Camino de Santiago

HIC E
ST COR
PUS DI
VI IACO
BI APOS
TOLI E
T ISPA
NIARV
PATRO
NI
MAYER

Rev. Greg J. Markey

DISCOVERING
—THE—
CAMINO
DE SANTIAGO

*A Priest's Journey to the
Tomb of St. James*

SOPHIA INSTITUTE PRESS
Manchester, New Hampshire

Copyright © 2023 by Rev. Greg J. Markey
First published © 2011 by Roman Catholic Books
Printed in the United States of America. All rights reserved.

Cover by LUCAS Art & Design / Jenison, MI

Cover image: *Calzada romana y valle de la Fuenfría; Mapa de las provincias de España*

Frontispiece: *Santiago Apóstol en la Capilla Mayor* by Enrique Mayer Castro, 1924. Wikimedia Commons.

Unless otherwise noted, biblical references in this book are taken from the *New Revised Standard Version Bible: Catholic Edition*, copyright © 1989, 1993 National Council of the Churches of Christ in the United States of America. Used by permission. All rights reserved worldwide.

No part of this book may be reproduced, stored in a retrieval system, or transmitted in any form, or by any means, electronic, mechanical, photocopying, or otherwise, without the prior written permission of the publisher, except by a reviewer, who may quote brief passages in a review.

Sophia Institute Press
Box 5284, Manchester, NH 03108
1-800-888-9344
www.SophiaInstitute.com

Sophia Institute Press is a registered trademark of Sophia Institute.

paperback ISBN 979-8-88911-224-2

ebook ISBN 979-8-88911-225-9

Library of Congress Control Number: 2023952438

First printing

To the Blessed Virgin Mary
De Maria Numquam Satis

Contents

Foreword by Most Rev. Kevin C. Rhoades ix
Preface xvii
1. Introduction 3
2. The Story of Santiago 11
3. Historical Accuracy of the Story: Pope Leo XIII's Papal Bull
   Deus Omnipotens 31
4. El Camino de Santiago. 43
   Part 1: The Excitement of the Camino, June 23, 2009 45
   Part 3: The Grace of the Camino, July 8, 2009 71
   Part 4: The Rhythm of the Camino, July 19, 2009 90
   Part 5: The Fulfillment of the Camino, July 28, 2010. . . . 106
5. Conclusion. 121
Appendix 127
About the Author. 137

Foreword by Most Rev. Kevin C. Rhoades

———— 🐚 ————

During this Holy Year, I come among you as a pilgrim among pilgrims, in the company of all those who come here thirsting for faith in the Risen Christ, a faith proclaimed and transmitted with fidelity by the apostles, among whom was James the Great, who has been venerated at Compostela from time immemorial.

WITH THESE WORDS, POPE Benedict XVI greeted eight thousand faithful at an outdoor Mass in front of the Cathedral of Santiago de Compostela, Spain, on November 6, 2010. The Holy Father went on pilgrimage to the "House of Saint James" during the Holy Year of Compostela, a jubilee celebrated every year when the feast of Saint James, July 25, falls on a Sunday.

The famous Cathedral of Santiago de Compostela, in northwest Spain, contains the remains of the apostle St. James the Great. Inside the cathedral, before the outdoor Mass in the plaza, Pope Benedict prayed before the tomb and, following the traditional pilgrim custom, embraced his statue.

For over one thousand years, pilgrims have traveled to Santiago de Compostela. It was one of the major destinations of Christian pilgrims in the Middle Ages, second only to Rome and Jerusalem.

In this book, Fr. Greg Markey shares the experience of his pilgrimage along the historic *Camino de Santiago,* the *Way of Saint James,* one of many old pilgrimage routes from all over Europe to the Cathedral of Santiago. Fr. Markey's account is more than a travelogue as he shares his faith, his challenges, his encounters, and his hopes while walking the way to Compostela. Fr. Markey's faith shines through as he prays each day of the pilgrimage and bears witness to other pilgrims of the "faith proclaimed and transmitted with fidelity by the apostles." With both wit and wisdom, Fr. Markey describes the experience of the contemporary pilgrim to Santiago de Compostela. He shares his personal experience of meeting other pilgrims: fellow Catholics, practicing and non-practicing; other Christians; and people struggling to believe—all "thirsty," as Pope Benedict stated, "for faith in the Risen Christ."

Reading this book, one recognizes that Fr. Markey's pilgrimage was not simply a private devotional exercise. As a priest with the first task of preaching the Gospel, he evangelized and catechized along the way. He sought to help other pilgrims discover the joy of encountering Christ, the joy of St. James and the apostles and all those who share the Catholic Faith "that comes to us from the apostles." Fr. Markey was also inspired during the journey by the faith of other pilgrims and by the kindness of those who assisted him along the way.

Foreword by Most Rev. Kevin C. Rhoades

At the welcome ceremony at the international airport in Santiago de Compostela, Pope Benedict spoke the following words:

> In his deepest being, man is always on a journey, ever in search of truth. The Church shares this profound human desire and herself sets out, accompanying humanity in its yearning for complete fulfillment. At the same time, the Church pursues her own interior journey which, through faith, hope, and love, leads her to become a transparent sign of Christ for the world. This is her mission and her path: to be among men and women an ever greater presence of Christ "whom God made our wisdom, our righteousness and sanctification and redemption" (1 Corinthians 1:30).

Fr. Markey's account of his pilgrimage reveals the truth of the Holy Father's words as he met and conversed with people of many different nations, all "in search of truth." They walked together to the tomb of an apostle of Jesus. With different needs and hopes, they were united in the human desire for fulfillment.

The Church, as Pope Benedict reminds us, accompanies humanity on this journey of life. She is not a bystander. She does so as the bearer of "Good News," proclaiming in word and deed the Kingdom of God, definitively established through the Cross of Jesus Christ. St. James, along with Sts. Peter and John, experienced a foretaste of that Kingdom at the Transfiguration of Jesus. They heard God the Father designate Jesus "as his Beloved Son," instructing them to "listen to him." It is in listening to the Son of God that we find truth, meaning, and joy in life. In Him, our hunger is satisfied and our thirst is quenched. The Church offers to all thirsty and hungry pilgrims the bread of life and the cup of salvation. The Church proclaims Jesus Christ as the way, the truth, and the life.

We are all pilgrims on this earth, in exile as it were, since our true and lasting home is Heaven. Sacred Scripture gives abundant testimony to this truth. It is foreshadowed in the Old Testament where the people of God journeyed in the Exodus to the Promised Land. Later in their history, they were uprooted from their homeland and transported to exile in Babylon. How many of the psalms recount the people's longing to escape their exile in a foreign land and return to Jerusalem, their true home! For the Church, the new people of God, our longing is for the new Jerusalem, our heavenly homeland.

It is important to see our life on earth as a pilgrimage to Heaven, to take seriously the teaching of Jesus that we are *in the world* but are not to be *of the world.* In speaking to the disciples of His imminent departure from this world, Jesus assured them that He was going to prepare a place for them in His Father's house (John 14:2–3). These words are also addressed to those who believe in Him.

St. Paul often reminded the communities he founded to recognize their pilgrim status on earth and to hope for Heaven. He told the early Christians: "Our commonwealth is in heaven" (Phil. 3:20). And he wrote about his own desire to live forever with Christ in Heaven: "My desire is to depart and be with Christ" (Phil. 1:23). St. Paul yearned to be in Heaven with Christ, yet he did not shirk his earthly mission. This yearning for Heaven did not diminish his apostolic zeal in this life. Instead, it increased it! His desire to be with Christ forever was the driving force that animated his incredible missionary work and urged him always to do more for Christ and His gospel. It is this desire that can motivate us to fulfill our earthly responsibilities, to live life to the full, to obey God's commandments, to do good works, to be faithful to our vocations, and to serve the Lord with dedication and love.

In preparation for the Great Jubilee of the Year 2000, Pope John Paul II wrote:

> The whole of the Christian life is like a great "pilgrimage to the house of the Father," whose unconditional love for every human creature, and in particular for the "prodigal son," we discover anew each day. This pilgrimage takes place in the heart of each person, extends to the believing community and then reaches to the whole of humanity. (Tertio millennio adveniente 49)

Before he died, Pope John Paul II was profoundly aware that his earthly pilgrimage was coming to an end. On the last day of his life on earth (April 2, 2005), the vigil of Divine Mercy Sunday, he was heard to say: "Let me go to the house of the Father." He lived his life on earth as a pilgrimage to the house of the Father, to Heaven. He served the Church until the very end. Pope John Paul II taught all of us how to live and how to die: in the light of faith and with hope in Christ.

As you read Fr. Markey's account of his pilgrimage to Santiago de Compostela, it is good to remember that our Christian life is a pilgrimage to our Father's house, a pilgrimage of faith, hope, and charity. The final goal of our life's pilgrimage is what gives meaning and value to our earthly life. It is what inspires us to work for good and to persevere in living our baptismal promises each day.

Fr. Markey's witness on his pilgrimage to Compostela reminds all of us of our duty to bear witness to the life, death, and Resurrection of Jesus Christ. This is the mission and task of the Church, "to be an ever-greater presence of Christ," as Pope Benedict said in the cathedral of Santiago. This is the greatest contribution we can ever make to our fellow pilgrims in the journey of life, our society, and our world.

We are to be a leaven for the growth of God's Kingdom on earth through lives of faith, hope, and charity. We are to seek to overcome evil with good and to practice the corporal and spiritual works of mercy. We do not flee from the world or our earthly responsibilities. Instead, we seek to transform the world with the power of love, *God's* love, the love that brings reconciliation and true peace. We cannot do this by our own power. We act with the power of the Holy Spirit who dwells within us, the grace of God that enables us to serve the building of His Kingdom on earth.

As the Holy Eucharist sustained Fr. Markey on his arduous walk to Compostela, the Eucharist gives us the strength and energy we need to persevere in our faith and in our mission. The Holy Eucharist is the food for our earthly pilgrimage and the pledge of our future glory.

At the Mass in front of the Cathedral of Santiago de Compostela, Pope Benedict said to the faithful:

> Brothers and sisters, today we are called to follow the example of the apostles, coming to know the Lord better day by day and bearing clear and valiant witness to His gospel. We have no greater treasure to offer to our contemporaries.

May those who read this book enjoy the pilgrim's story. May it be an encouragement to all on the Christian pilgrimage of life!

+Kevin C. Rhoades
Bishop of Fort Wayne-South Bend

Camino Frances: The most popular pilgrimage route across northern Spain

Preface

THIS SECOND EDITION OF *Discovering the Camino de Santiago* manifests the continuing growth and interest—particularly here in the United States—in the ancient pilgrimage to the tomb of St. James. It has been fifteen years since I walked the Camino, and the number of pilgrims traveling to the tomb of Santiago has only increased. Certainly, part of the reason I wrote this book was that so few people in the United States in 2009 were familiar with the Camino de Santiago. According to the statistics released by the pilgrim office, 147,254 pilgrims walked the Camino that year, with fewer than 2 percent of those pilgrims being from the United States. Americans were then just a small minority of the pilgrims compared with the number from other countries.

Since then, numerous articles, books, and movies have been produced in English, with the result that the number of American pilgrims has dramatically increased. In 2023, a record number of 446,035 pilgrims completed the Camino, and the number from the United States was 32,069, second only to Spain. It is a remarkable movement of grace and a testament to the faith in our country that, outside of Spain, more pilgrims from the United States walked the Camino last year than from any European country. This is the first time this has ever happened.

Please note that this book was originally written to my parishioners when I was pastor of St. Mary Church in Norwalk, Connecticut. I am no longer the pastor there but currently serve as chaplain of Thomas Aquinas College. However, the narrative of the story should be understood within that original context. I have also added a few more stories in this latest edition that were not included in the original edition. In preparation for this 2024 edition, I went back and read through my handwritten journal that I carried while walking the Camino in 2009 and found more stories that I thought would be of interest.

St. James is still moving hearts and calling the faithful to come to his tomb to receive grace. I would like to thank Sophia Institute Press for taking an interest in publishing this edition. May it continue to bear fruit in inspiring people to take part in this ancient tradition of making the pilgrimage to the tomb of Santiago.

DISCOVERING THE
CAMINO DE SANTIAGO

Introduction

I FIRST HEARD OF the Camino de Santiago when I was in seminary. A fellow seminarian and friend, now Fr. Michael Black, had walked the Camino before entering seminary. He told me *the Way of St. James* is a traditional path of pilgrimage that leads to the city of Santiago de Compostela in northwest Spain where St. James is buried. I was intrigued as he told the many enchanting stories of his travels through Spain.

When I was ordained to the priesthood in 1999 for the Diocese of Bridgeport, my first pastor was a Spaniard, Msgr. Aniceto Villamide. He, too, had walked the Camino years ago as a seminarian in Spain. We often discussed his vivid memories over dinner. The more I heard about this ancient walk, the more I imagined someday I would dare to follow in his footsteps.

In the summer of 2009, I was blessed with the opportunity to take a sabbatical. This allotted time would be my opportunity to walk the famous Camino de Santiago as an act of thanksgiving for ten years of priesthood. My goal was to walk the 496-mile pilgrimage, starting in Saint-Jean-Pied-de-Port in southern France, giving myself enough time to arrive for his feast day on July 25. Here in this French village, three major Camino routes all converge, from Paris, Vézelay, and Le Puy, to form the most common Camino route entering Spain, the *Camino Frances*.

While on the pilgrimage, I emailed five stories back to my parish of St. Mary Church in Norwalk, Connecticut, from internet cafés along the Camino, keeping my parishioners informed of my whereabouts. Upon my return, I was pleasantly surprised at how far and wide these emailed stories traveled and how much enthusiasm they generated. Our diocesan communications director, Dr. Joseph McAleer, then decided to run some of the stories as articles in our diocesan newspaper over a number of months. Eventually, Roger McCaffrey of Roman Catholic Books contacted me and asked if he could publish the whole series. Many stories from my travel journal are included here that were not originally published in the articles. I am grateful to those who took such an interest in the grace-filled adventure.

If you visit any library, there are dozens of books about the Camino de Santiago. So the question immediately arises, "Why another book?" The simple answer is because I was quite surprised at how few Americans know about the Camino. There is also quite a bit of misinformation about the Camino de Santiago in English works. I have found the Spanish books have better historical information, especially the papal bull *Deus Omnipotens*, which I address in chapter 2 on the historical accuracy of Compostela.

While in Santiago de Compostela, the chancellor of the archdiocese, Don Elisardo Temperán Villaverde, gave

Introduction

me a Spanish copy of *Deus Omnipotens* printed in 1985,[1] celebrating the one-hundredth anniversary of the bull. What is perhaps even more compelling than the proclamation itself are the sixteen historical appendices written by the Jacobean scholars in this hundredth-anniversary edition. Their appendices give more precision to the pope's words. It is not uncommon for English books on Santiago de Compostela to doubt the authenticity of St. James's historical connection to the Iberian Peninsula; however, I have also never seen any of this valuable information from the bull and appendices published anywhere in English. While there will always be skeptics, *Deus Omnipotens* gives solid evidence that it is reasonable to hold that the sacred relics are truly in Compostela. Therefore, I think this brief summary of the papal bull in chapter 2 and the appendices is extremely valuable to English readers.

I also wanted to write a book about the Camino based on the perspective of a believer. Only a minority of the people on the Camino today are practicing Catholics, even though the story is rich in Catholic history. Furthermore, most of the books today about the Camino are written from a secular perspective. I write this book as a believer. I would like to encourage devotion to St. James, hoping that some would even consider walking the Camino as a means of growing in their faith and in order to give witness to the

---

[1] Leo XIII, *Roma y el Sepulcro de Santiago: La Bula "Deus Omnipotens" (1884)*, con notas históricas por José Guerra Campos, Obispo de Cuenca (Santiago de Compostela: Edición del Excmo. Cabildo de la S.A.M.I. Catedral, 1985).

Catholic Faith. My hope is that this book may help lead to a rediscovery of the Camino de Santiago and remind the faithful of what Catholic culture is all about.

In the United States, walking on pilgrimage for hundreds of miles is not a common occurrence, yet pilgrimages are very much part of the Catholic tradition. In fact, Jesus went on pilgrimage three times every year with the Holy Family, walking from Nazareth up to the Temple in Jerusalem for the three feasts of Passover, Pentecost, and the Feast of Booths.[2]

A pilgrimage is the journey a believer travels to a holy place to ask for pardon, beg a favor, or thank God for blessings received. As one pilgrim wrote, "It might seem all very superstitious to the scientifically sophisticated population of our modern Western world, but for centuries much of life in the Christian world revolved around relics, prayers, and pilgrimages. Our predecessors in the faith held firmly to three simple beliefs. One: God cares infinitely about us. Two: the saints know what we are up against and direct God's kind attention our way. And three: miracles happen."[3]

For Catholics, the most popular pilgrimages have been to venerate relics, the precious remains of a saint. Blessings and miracles are believed to emanate from them, a tradition that goes all the way back to the apostles themselves in Scripture: "And God did extraordinary miracles by the hands of

---

[2] Miriam Feinberg Vamosh, *Daily Life at the Time of Jesus* (Herzlia, Israel: Palphot Ltd., 1992), 30.

[3] Kevin A. Codd, *To the Field of Stars: A Pilgrim's Journey to Santiago de Compostela* (Grand Rapids, Michigan: William B. Eerdmans Publishing Company, 2008), xi.

Introduction

Paul, so that handkerchiefs or aprons were carried away from his body to the sick, and diseases left them and the evil spirits came out of them" (Acts 19:11–12). Tombs that contained the bones of saints became important pilgrimage sights in the early Church, particularly the catacombs in Rome, and this type of devotion remains an integral part of Catholic piety even to this day.

I would like to thank Fr. Donald Haggerty for his continual charity, wisdom, and patience. I would also like to thank my bishop, William E. Lori, for giving me his blessing on this pilgrimage and my dedicated staff at St. Mary Church, particularly Erlinda Zelaya, without whom none of this would be possible. I would also like to thank the parishioners of St. Mary Church, whose honor I have of serving as their pastor. Their continual prayers sustained me during the more trying moments of the Camino. I am grateful to my sister-in-law, Cathy Markey, for her detailed editing skills, and most of all to my devoted parents, who are always there for me on the Camino of life.

Lastly, I alone am responsible for any defects in translation or errors in historical notes. If anyone should grow in closer to the truth and love of God through this work, then may the praise go the Author and Fount of all graces.

Fr. Greg J. Markey
Pastor of Saint Mary Church, Norwalk, 2010

ONE

The Story of Santiago

SANTIAGO IS SPANISH FOR "St. James," and James is the anglicized version of the Hebrew name Jacob. Jacob was the third of the three great Patriarchs of the Old Testament: Abraham, Isaac, and Jacob, and from his descendants came the entire nation of Israel. Throughout the Hebrew Scriptures, the Lord refers to His chosen people as the "house of Jacob," (Isa. 2:5, Obad. 1:18) signifying the chosen people of God with whom He has made His covenant, and where His "remnant" dwells (Isa. 46:3). At the same time, they are a people on a journey "who seek the face of the God of Jacob" (Ps. 24:6).

When the Archangel Gabriel announced to the Virgin Mary that she would conceive the long-awaited Messiah, Gabriel prophesied, "He will reign over the house of Jacob for ever" (Luke 1:33). The literal meaning of this phrase is that the Messiah will reign over His people forever. Nonetheless, the spiritual sense of the phrase can be understood to prophesy a "house of James" where God will dwell until the end of time.

The story of the person of St. James, of course, begins with the Gospels. James and his brother, John, were sons of Zebedee and Mary Salome. They were a Jewish family who would have been looking forward to the coming of the Messiah. The family had a large fishing business on the Sea of Galilee, which required hired workers (Mark 1:20). James and John were "partners" with Peter as fishermen (Luke 5:10) and were present when Peter miraculously brought in a huge catch of fish at the command of Jesus. Jesus then called James and John as they were working on the edge of the Galilean Sea, mending their nets. The two brothers must have experienced a powerful surge of grace within their hearts because they immediately left everything and followed Him (Matt. 4:22). As disciples, they followed Jesus, witnessing His miracles firsthand and listening to Him proclaim the arrival of the Kingdom of God (Mark 1:15).

One night, Jesus spent the entire night in prayer and, the next morning, called twelve of His disciples "whom he named apostles" (Luke 6:13). James was chosen as one of the apostles. As an apostle, James travelled with Jesus for three years listening to Him teach parables to the crowds and then had private time with the Lord afterward so as to learn the deeper meaning of these parables. Jesus told these apostles, "To you it has been given to know the secrets of the kingdom of heaven" (Matt. 13:11). James and the apostles were also given "power and authority over all demons and to cure diseases" (Luke 9:1), and they "went through the villages, preaching the gospel and healing everywhere" (Luke 9:6). To these twelve men, many of whom were simple fishermen, was entrusted the most important mission in the history of the world: the preaching of the gospel and the founding of the Catholic Church for the salvation of the world.

Of all the twelve apostles, Peter, James, and John were the closest to the Lord, as evidenced by Jesus inviting them to witness certain miracles separate from the other apostles: the raising of Jairus's daughter (Mark 5:35–43), Jesus' miraculous Transfiguration on Mount Tabor (Matt. 17:1–8), and Jesus' agony in the garden (Matt. 26:36–37).

Each of the three received a special grace from this privileged relationship with the Lord. Christ appointed St. Peter to be the leader and the rock upon which the Church would be built (Matt. 16:18–19). St. John became "the beloved disciple" of the Lord and received the most precious gift from Him: to be the caretaker of His mother, the Blessed Virgin Mary (John 19:26–27). St. James would receive his gift later as the missionary to Spain with the privilege of being the first of the apostles to give his life for Christ.[4]

James and his brother, John, also received the name "sons of thunder" (Mark 3:17) from the Lord, perhaps because of their impetuous behavior. In the Gospels, the

[4] An argument can be made that St. Andrew had a more important role than St. James since he was called before St. James (Matt. 4:18; John 1:40). However, Scripture says little about St. Andrew (John 6:8), and he was not part of the three miracles mentioned above. In the four listings of the apostles in Scripture, St. Andrew is listed prior to St. James twice (Matt. 10:2; Luke 6:14) and St. James is listed prior to St. Andrew twice (Mark 3:17; Acts 1:13). St. Andrew also has the distinction of having his name listed two times in the centuries old 1962 Roman Missal, both in the Canon and in the *Libera nos*.

brothers ask the Lord to send lightning down upon the unwelcoming Samaritans (Luke 9:54); they also ask to be seated at the Lord's right and left when He comes in glory, ahead of the other apostles (Mark 10:35–40). The two were rightly corrected by the Lord for their haughty attitudes.

The fullness of James's undertaking as an apostle was revealed to him at the Last Supper. On that night which would forever change the world, Jesus ordained James and the rest of the apostles as bishops,[5] consecrated the Eucharist for the first time, and commanded them to "do this in remembrance of me" (Luke 22:19). Jesus also gave them an example of charitable service by washing their feet (John 13:5). James's larger mission for the remainder of his life was now clear: in a spirit of charity, offer the Holy Sacrifice of the Mass and ordain more bishops so that the Holy Mass would be perpetually offered until the end of time.

Yet the intense joy of the evening was shattered when the Jewish authorities arrested Jesus. As Jesus had predicted, at this crucial moment, James and the apostles "all forsook him, and fled" (Mark 14:50). They still lacked the gifts of the Holy Spirit and were not yet ready for their mission. Only John, who had the deepest love for the Lord, had the strength to return and witness Jesus' terrible Crucifixion and death (John 19:26).

The apostles hid in fear and sadness until Jesus rose from the dead on the third day. He appeared to them numerous times over a forty-day period, sometimes rebuking them "for

---

[5] Council of Trent, chap. X, canon II.

their unbelief and hardness of heart" (Mark 16:14), and other times encouraging them for the mission now at hand. Before ascending into Heaven, Jesus commanded James and the other apostles to "go therefore and make disciples of all nations" (Matt. 28:19) and to be His witnesses "to the end of the earth" (Acts 1:8).

They would now have to wait for the coming of the Holy Spirit at Pentecost to fulfill all that Jesus was asking them. While preparing for this manifestation of God's spirit, "Peter and John and James," along with the rest of the remaining apostles, "devoted themselves to prayer, together with the women and Mary the mother of Jesus" (Acts 1:13–14). Surely during this contemplative time alone with the Blessed Virgin, James deepened his love and devotion for the Mother of Jesus.

When Pentecost came, the apostles were "filled with the Holy Spirit and began to speak in other tongues" (Acts 2:4). They built up the Church in Palestine, preaching, baptizing, and offering the Holy Sacrifice of the Mass. Eventually, each of them travelled in different directions across the globe to fulfill Christ's command of consecrating new bishops and priests, offering Jesus' Body and Blood at the sacrifice of the Mass, and forgiving sins.

Tradition states that James went to "the end of the earth," as they understood the end of the earth at that time: he went all the way to the Iberian Peninsula, modern-day Spain and Portugal. Although James's mission is not specifically mentioned in the Scriptures, it may have been immediately after the martyrdom of St. Stephen. Scripture states, "On that day a great persecution arose against the church in Jerusalem; and they were all scattered throughout the region" (Acts 8:1).

After travelling through sections of Spain, St. James's words were not penetrating the hearts of the Spaniards, who were given over to the Roman gods. In the year 40, while in the city of Zaragoza (Caesaraugusta), St. James prayed, asking for the strength to continue, and the Lord sent not an angel but His Mother, the Blessed Virgin Mary, *en carne mortal* (in mortal flesh).[6] Here, she appeared on a pillar, encouraging his faith and hope, and asked for a church to be built at this location. This appearance is the only alleged bilocation ever recorded of the Blessed Virgin Mary and manifests a profound bond between St. James and Our Lady. In obedience, St. James built a church dedicated to the Blessed Virgin in Zaragoza. Today, a magnificent basilica under the title of *Nuestra Señora del Pilar* stands over the original location, where she is honored as the patroness of Spain. The basilica is considered the oldest church dedicated to Our Lady in the world.

St. James later returned to Jerusalem in the year 44. He was beheaded on March 25 by Herod Agrippa[7] and became the first apostle to die for the Faith. "About that time Herod the king laid violent hands upon some who belonged to the church. He killed James the brother of John with the sword" (Acts 12:1–2).

---

[6] Mariano Nougués Secali, *Historia, Crítica y Apologética de La Virgen Nuestra Señora del Pilar de Zaragoza y de su Templo y Tabernáculo desde el Siglo I hasta Nuestras Días* (Madrid: D. Alejandro Gómez Fuentenebro, 1862), 21–22.

[7] Padre Juan de Mariana, *Historia de España* (Madrid: Una Sociedad de Literatos, 1844), 19.

Ten of the other apostles would also eventually follow St. James as martyrs, with only St. John dying a natural death. According to the early Church historian Eusebius, the man who brought the charges up to have St. James condemned was so moved by the saint's testimony that he, too, converted to the Faith. "So they were both taken away together, and on the way he asked James to forgive him. James thought for moment; then he said, 'I wish you peace', and kissed him. So both were beheaded at the same time."[8]

There are two mystics approved by the Catholic Church who have elaborated on this missionary activity of St. James to Spain and the special visits he received from the Blessed Virgin Mary. Venerable Mary of Agreda, the seventeenth-century Spanish mystic, wrote extensively about St. James's dangerous missionary work in Spain, the great love between this apostle and Our Lady, his many miracles in Spain, the origin of the sanctuary of the Pillar of Saragossa, the ordination of the first Spanish bishops, and his violent death.[9]

Blessed Anne Catherine Emmerich, the nineteenth-century German mystic, also received visions about St. James's apostolic work in Spain and his inspiring martyrdom in Jerusalem.[10]

[8] Eusebius, *The History of the Church*, trans. G. A. Williamson (New York: Barnes and Noble Publishing, 1995), 81–82.
[9] Mary of Agreda, *City of God: The Coronation,* trans. Fiscar Marison (Chicago: The Theopolitan, 1914), 297–304, 322–333, 349, 349–352, 357–364.
[10] Anne Catherine Emmerich, *The Life of Christ and Biblical Revelations*, vol. 4, trans. an American Nun (Rockford, Illinois: Tan Books and Publishers, Inc.), 448–450.

Fearing the Jews would further desecrate his body, two of St. James's disciples, Athanasius and Theodoro, took the saint's body from Jerusalem back to Spain by sea and arrived on July 25,[11] the date that would later become his feast day. They buried him in the northwest corner of the Iberian Peninsula, modern-day Galicia. Over time, through the breakdown of the Roman Empire, the barbarian invasion, and then the Muslim invasion, the burial site was overgrown, becoming more obscure.

Nonetheless, Spain's faithful maintained the presence of St. James in their hearts, and the Lord would not allow the precious relics of this apostle to be forgotten. In the early ninth century, a hermit from the area named Pelagius witnessed a mysterious light emanating from a field one evening. He rushed to tell the local bishop of Iria Flavia, Teodomiro, who immediately had the area cleared of brush. There, they found a small chapel with three tombs inside. Bishop Teodomiro declared they had found St. James's remains in the larger tomb and his two faithful disciples, Athanasius and Theodora, in the smaller tombs. He had a chapel built to house the relics there in Compostela, or known in Latin as *campus stellae*, translated as "star field." Others argue the name comes from the Latin *componere*, to "mix" or "bury," because it is the burial place of St. James.[12]

When the king of Asturias, Alphonsus II, heard of the discovery, he came on pilgrimage from Oviedo and ordered

---

[11] Mariana, *Historia de España*, 19.
[12] Leo XIII, *Roma y el Sepulcro de Santiago*, appendix VI, 63.

a church be erected over the tomb. He also arranged for the building of a monastery nearby, and so the pilgrims began to come. The discovery of the tomb of St. James at that time proved to be a crucial ingredient in the *Reconquista*, or reconquering of Spain. In 712, Muslims crossed over from North Africa and began their invasion of Spain, slaying thousands of Catholics in city after city and deporting many into slavery.[13] Churches were turned into mosques,[14] and the invaders successfully secured almost the entire peninsula for hundreds of years. While there were periods of cultural exchange between the Catholics and Muslims and times of leniency, those Catholics who remained were forced to pay the *jizya*, or tax, as second-class citizens under Sharia Law.[15] In addition, the ninth century came to be called the "great era of the martyrs in Spain" due to the large number of saints killed at the hands of Muslim rulers.[16]

The *Reconquista* began in 722 with the victorious Battle of Covadonga in the northern region of Asturias. The Reconquista took a decisive step in 844 when one of the Catholic kings, Ramiro I, refused to give the Moors the annual tribute of one hundred virgins. The Battle of Calvijo

---

[13] Bat Ye'or, *The Decline of Eastern Christianity under Islam: From Jihad to Dhimmitude*, trans. Miriam Kochan and David Littman (Madison: Fairleigh Dickenson University Press, 1996), 49–50.
[14] Ibid., 83.
[15] Ibid., 77–78.
[16] Herbert J. Thurston and Donald Attwatter, eds., *Butler's Lives of the Saints*, vol. 4 (Allen, Texas: Christian Classics, 1996), 178.

ensued.[17] The Catholics were outnumbered, but a visionary soldier appeared—St. James on horseback with a sword in hand. Ramiro claimed victory, freeing the Spaniards from this horrible form of a tax, and this vision of Santiago on horseback, Santiago Matamoros (St. James the Moorslayer), now became the rallying point for the Reconquista. Soon thereafter, images and statues of the apostle warrior appeared in churches throughout the region. Confraternities among princes and soldiers also sprang up promising payment to Santiago in thanksgiving for military victories.[18]

The Muslim fear of Santiago Matamoros was characterized by the terrifying military march led by the Muslim ruler Almanzor in 997, who obliterated many populated areas through northern Spain. Almanzor's intention was to destroy the cathedral in Santiago, knowing that this cathedral was the source of strength for the Catholic people. Almanzor nearly succeeded, razing the city and reducing it to ashes, but he was ultimately thrown back in a humiliating defeat.[19]

Santiago Matamoros is alleged to have appeared more than twenty times at decisive battles all over the peninsula[20] before the Reconquista was complete in 1492, driving the last Muslim ruler out of Granada. Understandably Santiago Matamoros became known as the protector of Spain, and to this day he remains an important part of Spanish history.

[17] Louis Cardaillac, *Santiago Apóstol: El Santo De Los Dos Mundos* (Jalisco: El Colegio de Jalisco, 2002), 40–41.
[18] Ibid., 42–43.
[19] Leo XIII, *Roma y el Sepulcro de Santiago*, 24–25.
[20] Cardaillac, *Santiago Apóstol*, 40.

The Story of Santiago

Curiously, a mystical warrior on horseback fighting for the Lord is also present in Sacred Scripture. The Second Book of Maccabees recalls the story of the Greeks who, in the second century before Christ, were attempting to despoil the Temple in Jerusalem. Heliodorus boldly attempted to violate the holiness of the Temple by entering the treasury when he was violently thrown back by a fearsome rider on a horse. "For there appeared to them a magnificently caparisoned horse, with a rider of frightening mien, and it rushed furiously at Heliodor'us and struck at him with its front hoofs. Its rider was seen to have armor and weapons of gold. Two young men also appeared to him, remarkably strong, gloriously beautiful and splendidly dressed, who stood on each side of him and scourged him continuously, inflicting many blows on him. When he suddenly fell to the ground and deep darkness came over him, his men took him up and put him on a stretcher and carried him away" (2 Macc. 3:25–28). Certainly, there is precedent for the Lord using a mystical warrior on horseback to defend His holy ground.

According to ancient traditions, the Catholic emperor Charlemagne, king of the Franks, also played an integral role in the devotion to St. James, linking the Reconquista with the pilgrim route from the rest of Europe. In the twelfth-century document *Codex Calixtinus*, Charlemagne received a dream where he saw in the heavens a long belt of stars that started on the northern coast of the Frisian Sea and then extended down over Germany, Italy, France, and all the way across northern Spain to Galicia.

While meditating on the vision, a horseman appeared to him who explained, "I am St. James the Apostle, disciple of

Christ, son of Zebedee, whose body rests ignored in Galicia, which still remains under the yoke of the Saracens."

The apostle then revealed to Charlemagne the meaning of the vision and his mission. "The way of stars that you have contemplated in the sky signifies that from this land to Galicia, you must go with a great army to fight the pagans, and free my path and land, and visit my basilica and my tomb. And after you, many peoples will go on pilgrimage from sea to sea, begging pardon for their sins, and announcing the praises of the Lord. Truly, they will go on pilgrimage from your times until the end of the present age."[21]

Charlemagne descended upon Spain in 778, battling the Muslim occupiers and clearing a path for the pilgrims who could then safely travel to the apostle's tomb. From this crusade developed the famous *Song of Roland*, the oldest existing epic poem in French, describing the tragic loss in Roncesvalles of Roland, one of the leading knights in Charlemagne's army, as they returned from battle. Ancient markers commemorating the stirring battle still lie along the Camino today.

With the Reconquista clearing northern Spain of Muslim rule in the ninth century, the "Camino de Santiago" grew to become an enormously popular pilgrimage route. Pilgrims followed paths from France, Germany, Italy, and beyond, all hoping to reach the tomb of St. James. Hostels, religious houses, and even towns grew up along the way to care for the large number of pilgrims. Countless saints, nobility, and lay people walked the way to St. James, including St. Francis of

[21] Ibid., 52–53.

Assisi, St. Bridget of Sweden, and St. Isabel of Portugal.[22] Popes wrote numerous ecclesial documents granting indulgences and encouraging the faithful to go on pilgrimage to Santiago.[23] It eventually became one of the three most important pilgrimage sights in Europe, along with Jerusalem (where Jesus was crucified) and Rome (where Sts. Peter and Paul were martyred). Pope Pius XII beautifully described the significance of the pilgrimage to Santiago de Compostela when he wrote, "After the Tabernacle, where Our Lord Jesus Christ lives, truly present though invisible; and after the Holy Sepulcher, which preserves the traces of His passage on this earth; and after Rome, which safeguards the glorious tombs of the Princes of the Apostles, there is perhaps no place where such great numbers of devoted pilgrims have gathered over the centuries as the historic capital of Galicia, Santiago de Compostela, where according to an ancient tradition, the relics of St. James the Great are to be found."[24]

In fulfillment of the prophecy spoken to Charlemagne, the original cathedral of Santiago de Compostela could not keep up with the many pilgrims arriving each day from all over Europe, and it eventually had to be replaced with a larger one. Bishop Pedro Muniz consecrated the current

---

[22] Leo XIII, *Roma y el Sepulcro de Santiago*, appendix VII, 71. A total of twenty-seven saints who are known to have walked the Camino during the Middle Ages is listed here.
[23] Ibid., appendix XII, 95–104.
[24] Pius XII, *Dear Newlyweds: Pope Pius XII Speaks to Married Couples*, trans. James F. Murray and Bianca M. Murray (Kansas City: Sarto House), 234.

cathedral on April 4, 1211, after more than one hundred years of construction.

Many fascinating cultural achievements developed during the medieval period, such as historic monasteries, handcrafted bridges for the pilgrims, and various artistic expressions of the pilgrimage. Dante's *Paradise* included Santiago's Camino "at whose Galician tomb the pilgrims pray."[25] He also pointed out that "palmers" are those who go to the Holy Land, "romers" are those who go to Rome, "but pilgrims in the strict sense are only those who go to the house of St. James."[26] Centuries-old Camino markers are still scattered throughout the cities and villages of Western Europe today, pointing pilgrims from an age long past toward Santiago de Compostela.

Perhaps nothing is more mysterious than the invaluable twelfth-century manuscript *Codex Calixtinus*, also known as the *Liber Sancti Jacob*, which was discovered in the archives of Santiago. It contains a variety of information on the Camino de Santiago: ancient history and sermons, travel routes of the Camino pilgrims through Europe, and some of the earliest forms of polyphonic music known. Although it was originally attributed to Pope Calixtus II, scholars today still do not know the manuscript's origin or how it arrived at Santiago.[27]

The image of "St. James the Pilgrim" developed during this period: St. James is dressed in a broad-brimmed hat,

---

[25] Dante, *Paradise*, trans. Anthony Esolen (New York: The Modern Library, 2004), XXV v. 17–18.

[26] Dante, *Vita Nuova*, 40; quoted in Leo XIII, *Roma y el Sepulcro de Santiago*, appendix VII, 74.

[27] Susan Hellauer, *Miracles of Compostela: Plain-chant et polyphonies du Codex Calixtinus* (Burbank, California: Harmonia Mundi, 2008).

carrying a walking stick with a fastened gourd, and wearing a scallop shell.[28] The scallop shell has come to be the universal symbol of St. James the Pilgrim. There are different stories as to its origin. Some say the shell serves the pilgrim well for drinking water or should the need for Baptism arise. Others argue that it is the universal symbol because the early pilgrims continued onto the seacoast after visiting Compostela and picked up a shell before returning back to the heartland of Europe. There are also various legends, such as the knight who fell into the sea when St. James's remains arrived in Galicia in the first century; and through the intercession of St. James, he was miraculously saved, rising up out of the water covered with scallop shells.[29]

Perhaps the most convincing meaning of the scallop shell is that its converging ridges are a symbol of the many pilgrimage paths throughout Europe all converging on the city of Santiago de Compostela in fulfillment of Charlemagne's dream of the long belt of stars. For the last 1,200 years, pilgrims have made this journey to the tomb of St. James from sea to sea, and the pilgrims doing the Camino today still place the shell somewhere on their clothing as an official sign of their pilgrim status.

In sum, there are three important images of St. James that have developed over time: St. James the Apostle, Santiago Matamoros, and St. James the Pilgrim. Each of these images plays a vital role in a proper understanding of the Camino de Santiago.

[28] Cardaillac, *Santiago Apóstol*, 50.
[29] Hellauer, *Miracles of Compostela*.

Although the Camino grew less popular during the sixteenth and seventeenth centuries due to skepticism about relics and the critical spirit of the Protestant Reformation,[30] it still maintained a steady flow of pilgrims.[31] A strong renewal in the pilgrimage began again at the end of the nineteenth century with Pope Leo XIII's papal bull *Deus Omnipotens* in 1884.[32] The pope confirmed the sacred relics of St. James in Compostela and encouraged the faithful around the world to go on pilgrimage to the apostle's tomb. Angelo Roncalli, the future St. John XXIII, walked the Camino in 1908 as a young priest, and visited again as a Cardinal in 1954.[33] St. Josemaria Escrivá also made the journey to the tomb of St. James several times during his life; the first occasion was in 1938.[34]

A great revival in the pilgrimage to Santiago came through the influence of St. John Paul II when he visited Compostela in 1982. It was the first time a pope had ever visited Santiago. He then visited again when World Youth Day was held there in 1989. Furthermore, in 1993 UNESCO (United Nations Educational, Scientific and Cultural Organization) placed the Camino de Santiago on the list of World Heritage Sites, thereby increasing its

[30] Cardaillac, *Santiago Apóstol*, 110–111.
[31] Leo XIII, *Roma y el Sepulcro de Santiago*, appendix VII, 71–72.
[32] Ibid., appendix XIV, 119.
[33] Cardaillac, *Santiago Apóstol*, 113, 121.
[34] Luis Cano, San Josemaria, Peregrino de Santiago, Conferencia pronunciada en el Simposio Internacional "Grandes protagonistas de la peregrinación a Compostela", organizado por la Asociación Social y Cultural Porta do Camino en la sede del Instituto Teológico Compostelano, Aprii 20, 2010.

prestige. In 1999, a record eight million pilgrims came for the Jubilee year,[35] which occurs whenever the feast of St. James, July 25, falls on a Sunday. The Holy Doors of the cathedral are then opened, granting special graces to the pilgrims.

Most recently, Pope Benedict XVI visited Santiago during the Jubilee Year of 2010, drawing huge crowds and media coverage from around the world. On arriving at St. James's tomb, he stated: "In this Holy Year of Compostela, I too, as the Successor of Peter, wished to come in pilgrimage to the 'House of St. James.'"

Today, the Camino de Santiago is one of the most ancient manifestations of popular religious devotion in Europe and in the world. There are still hundreds of thousands of pilgrims coming to Compostela from many countries and of various religions, all seeking an opportunity to reflect on the larger questions of life, knowing they will endure many hardships along the way. Few pilgrims ever arrive disappointed. It is revealing that Jesus Himself, while on pilgrimage during His earthly life, and "wearied as he was with his journey," stopped at "Jacob's well" (John 4:6) to be refreshed.

The ancient promises of the pilgrimage are well summarized in the *Codex Calixtinus:* "The most holy power of the Apostle's body, transferred from the region of Jerusalem, miraculously shines forth in Galicia. There in the Basilica of St. James, God frequently performs miracles for

---

[35] Cardaillac, *Santiago Apóstol*, 114.

their edification: the sick come and are cured, the blind see the light, the crippled rise, the dumb speak, the possessed are freed from the devil, the sorrowful are consoled; and what is most important are the whispering prayers of the faithful who leave behind the heavy burden of their crimes, being freed from their slavery to sin."[36]

---

[36] Quoted in Ibid., 63.

TWO

Historical Accuracy of the Story: Pope Leo XIII's Papal Bull Deus Omnipotens

—— 🐚 ——

ARE THE REMAINS OF St. James the Apostle truly in Compostela? While there have been countless pilgrims through the years going on pilgrimage to Santiago, witnessing miracles and having inspiring stories to tell, questions remain as to whether the relics of St. James are truly there in Spain.

For example, the Scriptures make no reference to any connection between St. James and the Iberian Peninsula.

Furthermore, how is it possible that the sacred relics were apparently "hidden" for hundreds of years, only to be discovered in the ninth century?

But answers do exist. It is hard to conceive how millions of faithful people throughout history, from around the world, would be inspired to make such sacrifices in order to arrive at the tomb if St. James's sacred relics were not there. While this may be a compelling answer, the question still merits deeper examination.

It is important to recognize that primary historical sources from first-century Europe are not common. That written records of Santiago's trip have never been discovered is not proof he did not evangelize the Iberian Peninsula. Certain modern critics have become accustomed to dismissing entire sections of Santiago's long history, such as the story of the tragic death of Charlemagne's knight Roland in the *Song of Roland*, simply because they cannot find other historical sources to support the tradition. However, as historians say, "Absence of proof is not proof of absence." When it comes to ancient history, local traditions are often more reliable sources than written records.

At the end of the nineteenth century, Pope Leo XIII took up this question of whether the remains of St. James in Santiago are authentic. It is worth noting that prior to Pope Leo XIII, there were already 340 papal bulls from seventy popes about the pilgrimage site of Santiago, beginning in the fourteenth century.[37] Pope Leo XIII brought together a commission in 1879 to examine the historical evidence and to exhume the bones from the tomb, attempting to confirm the authenticity of the relics. The findings of that commission were published in Pope Leo XIII's papal bull *Deus Omnipotens* on November 1, 1884. A brief summary of the bull is presented here along with excerpts from the sixteen historical appendices written by Jacobean scholars published in the hundredth anniversary edition. All the quotations are taken from this edition, and the translation is my own.

The first question to consider is whether St. James ever preached in Spain. As noted, the Scriptures are silent on this issue. However, Church Fathers from the fourth and fifth

---

[37] Leo XIII, *Roma y el Sepulcro de Santiago*, 8.

centuries (St. Jerome, St. Hillary of Poitiers, St. Ephraim of Syria, and the historian Eusebius) explicitly mention Spain as one of the lands where the apostles preached.[38] Could it be the Church Fathers were referring to St. Paul's preaching in Spain since it is commonly understood that St. Paul also preached in parts of Spain? This would not have been St. Jerome's understanding, because he writes the Holy Spirit ordained that "each one of the 12 apostles was buried in the region where he evangelized and taught."[39] St. Jerome knew very well that St. Paul was buried in Rome.

History is clear that Spain had been evangelized right from the early centuries. In the year 180, St. Irenaeus of Lyon writes that Iberia had already been evangelized, "having received this preaching and this faith ... (and) carefully preserves it."[40] Furthermore, in the year 324, the Church in Spain held its first Church council with the Council of Elvira, and nineteen bishops from all over the Iberian Peninsula attended it. Who was it that produced such a strong foundation for the Church in Spain so early in the Church's history?

In the sixth and seventh centuries, there were biographies of the apostles, written by such illustrious men as St. Isidore of Seville, which expressly state the apostle St. James was a preacher of the Gospel in "Spain and Western Places."[41] From the eighth century until the Middle Ages, the references only became more numerous. Therefore, although it is not possible

[38] Ibid., appendix I, 39.
[39] Ibid., appendix I, 40.
[40] *Against Heresies*, I, x, 2.
[41] Leo XIII, *Roma y el Sepulcro de Santiago*, appendix I, 40.

using modern historical-critical methods to verify whether St. James did in fact preach in Spain, the Faith was firm in the Iberian Peninsula from the earliest centuries, and tradition passed down from generation to generation in Spain held that St. James was the founder of this church.

The next question is whether the remains in the tomb at Santiago de Compostela are truly those of St. James. The transfer of the remains by his disciples, Athanasius and Theodoro, is retold in *Deus Omnipotens* as an accepted tradition. One of the footnotes in the bull points out: "It is important to remember that, from the time of the Phoenician expansion, there was a very intense navigation between the coasts of the eastern Mediterranean and the coasts of Galicia, principally to search for metals on the Canary Islands."[42] This ancient trade route would have been the most likely means of travel for not only Athanasius and Theodoro but also St. James himself.

Modern excavations beneath the Basilica of St. James reveal a great deal of important information, filling in the eight-hundred-year gap from the arrival of his sacred relics in the first century to their discovery in the ninth century. The original ossuary containing the bones of St. James dates from the Roman period in the first century.[43] Along with the ossuary was discovered "a large Christian cemetery, with remains that range from the third century (in some cases the second) until the seventh century."[44] This would concur with

---

[42] Ibid., 21.
[43] Ibid., appendix II, 44.
[44] Ibid., appendix III, 50.

a third-century letter from St. Cyprian of Carthage who "rebuked the bishop of 'Galicia', of Astorga-Leon, who buried his children in a pagan cemetery."[45] Therefore, it is clear Christians had their own cemetery in Galicia during those first centuries.

Because of a silence in historical records from the fourth to the ninth century, it appears there was an interruption in the devotion at the tomb of St. James for centuries, perhaps due to a depopulation of northeastern Spain during that period. Nonetheless, the writings from such eminent authors as St. Isidore of Seville in the seventh century, who stated that St. James preached in Spain, and the eighth-century Iberian hymn *O Dei Verbum*, which invoked St. James as the evangelist and patron of Spain,[46] show that even before the rediscovery of the tomb in the ninth century, there was a definite understanding among the people of Spain that during this period, St. James was connected to their country.

The bull then gives a historical account of how in the early ninth century, under King Alphonsus II of Asturias, the sacred relics were discovered by "a very bright star ... indicating the place where the holy remains were buried." The local bishop of Iria Flavia, Teodomiro, "removed the debris of the chapel" and, after an investigation, identified the three tombs of St. James, Athanasius, and Theodoro.[47]

There was a tradition that stated Bishop Teodomiro moved his residence to be near the tomb and asked to be

---

[45] Ibid.
[46] Ibid., appendix XI, 91.
[47] Ibid., 23.

buried there. He died in 847 and was thought to have been buried near the tomb of St. James, but there was never any verification. This tradition was confirmed by recent discoveries of Bishop Teodomiro's tomb underneath the cathedral. "The excavations of 1956 have confirmed the ancient and widely discussed history, returning to us the tomb of the bishop, who died in 847."[48] Discoveries such as this give credence to the traditions that have been passed down for centuries.

Pope Leo XIII details the building of the first chapel and how the first pilgrims began to flock to the tomb of the apostle from all over Europe. When this hugely popular pilgrimage blossomed in Europe after the apparent discovery, certain obvious contradictions would have arisen if it were not authentic: "The clergy and faithful of Galicia, like those of the whole Church, were reading the Holy Scriptures (Acts 12:2) where the first martyr of the apostles had been killed in the Holy Land; and so they had to think that it was there where he was buried. In reality, if the transfer of the sacred relics was not known from antiquity, all the information related to the discovery of the ninth century would have been considered an incomprehensible invention."[49]

Furthermore, why were there no other claims to St. James's relics? From the earliest centuries, there were shrines in Palestine devoted to saints from apostolic times such as the other St. James, St. James the Lesser, and St. Stephen. If it was known that St. James the Greater was

---

[48] Ibid., appendix IV, 56.
[49] Ibid., appendix III, 52–53.

martyred in Palestine, why was there no devotion to him in that land? St. Jerome's claim that each of the apostles was buried in the land where he evangelized and taught begins to be more plausible.

Finally, Pope Leo XIII's commission performed the excavation of the bones in 1879. The bones had actually been hidden under the altar in a special ossuary by the canons of the cathedral in 1589 when the English were threatening to attack the basilica. After exploring various places underneath the cathedral, the ossuary was found by the commission and removed for detailed examination. The appendices describe how experts in human anatomy, archeology, and history were involved in an exhaustive study of the sacred relics.[50] These experts first concluded they were "bones belonging to the three skeletons of the masculine sex."[51] They then pursued the question of whether or not the relics found corresponded to St. James and his two disciples, Athanasius and Theodoro.

An important piece of information to the commission was the presentation of a twelfth-century certified relic of St. James that had been sent to the bishop of Pistoia, Italy, from Compostela. The relic of Pistoia was identified as "from the head: it is the mastoid process, and it still appears to be imbedded with blood, for having received the blow from the sword to do the decapitation."[52] This relic was

[50] Ibid., appendix XIII.
[51] Ibid., 29.
[52] Ibid., 26.

helpful in determining which of the three skeletons belong to St. James the Apostle.

Hundreds of bone fragments were meticulously analyzed, labeled, and documented. Experts in chemical bone analysis were able to determine that the bones were from "the first centuries of Christianity."[53] In addition, the studies showed that the age of the men at the time of their death was between "the second and final third physiological part of their lives."[54] The commission continued to work at overcoming certain doubts, inviting even more doctors to participate, before a consensus was reached in 1884. The testimony of the doctors and archeologists gave an affirmative decision regarding the relics' authenticity, and the official declaration was pronounced by Pope Leo XIII at the end of the bull:

> And today, wanting to confirm everything that was established in this decree with a most solemn act of ratification from our own Apostolic Authority, and following the steps of our Predecessors Benedict XIII, Pius VII and Pius IX, who issued a just declaration concerning the identity of the bodies of Saint Augustine, Bishop and Doctor, of Saint Francis of Assisi, of Saint Ambrose, Bishop and Doctor, and of the Saints Gervasio and Protasio, Martyrs; and having addressed all the doubts and

---

[53] Ibid., appendix XIII, 113.
[54] Ibid.

controversies, with scientific certainty, with the dictates of our Venerable Brother, the Cardinal Archbishop of Compostela, according to our own Apostolic Authority *(motu propio)*, We approve and confirm the identity of the most holy bodies of the Apostle Saint James the Greater and of his holy disciples Athanasius and Theodoro, and We declare that it would have perpetual force and value.

THREE

El Camino de Santiago

The following five parts are emails I sent to my parish while walking the Camino to be printed in the parish bulletin. Internet cafes are common in the towns and cities of Spain, and I was able to find some quiet time in the afternoons at these cafés to write these letters. I also kept a handwritten journal, recording the day's events, and the original emails were then expanded for this book using the reflections from the journal.

---- 🐚 ----

Part 1: The Excitement of the Camino, June 23, 2009

Fr. Markey walking west early in the morning on the Camino.

Although I boarded the plane in New York, I felt like I had just jumped out of one. With only the clothes I was wearing and a medium-size backpack filled with the most basic necessities, I was on my way. It was all supposed to last me for over a month. There was no turning back.

I have now been in Europe for a week and on the Camino for three days. I had one day in Paris and offered Mass in the beautiful church of Saint Sulpice. I saw the altar where the great Marian saint, St. Louis de Montfort, offered his first Holy Mass, and that gave me great courage in this foreign land.

That evening, I flew down to Lourdes for two days to relax and get over the jet lag. The next morning, I offered Mass at the simple grotto where Our Lady appeared to St. Bernadette in 1858. I then found a barber and asked for a crew cut, knowing that this would be the easiest way to travel over the next month. I did not know the word for "crew cut" in French, but I think the barber finally understood after some humorous moments.

This sabbatical is considered my annual retreat as well, so I brought along Cardinal Ratzinger's *Introduction to Christianity* to read and to be my "retreat master" for the month. As one person wrote of the book, "This is solid food that must be eaten slowly, but is very nourishing and worth the effort." So true. Spending time in Lourdes reading Cardinal Ratzinger (Pope Benedict XVI) and then having the beautiful Marian processions exemplifies the fullness of Catholicism. I then took a train through the Basque Country to Saint-Jean-Pied-de-Port, one of the traditional starting points in southern France, right at the base of the Pyrenees.

Getting off the train, I made my way up the narrow cobblestone streets to the hostel called *Esprit de le Chemin*. It was very busy and welcoming, reminding me a bit of a commune—free-spirited people who were happy to host you. It was my first Camino experience of sleeping in the same room with other people, on my own cot; I realized I better get used to this because I have at least another month of it. I then went to the *Accueil Saint Jacques* and officially registered as a pilgrim, obtaining my *credencial*, the "pilgrim passport" to be stamped along the path to Santiago.

The hostel offered a friendly dinner: a big bowl of cream of mushroom soup, fresh bread, with wine and water. There were about fifteen of us from many countries: Spain, France, Germany, Austria, Italy, and Canada. Some were biking the Camino, others were walking; some had already been on the Camino for weeks, but most were just starting. Before eating, someone asked if I would bless the meal, which I gladly did.

There was excitement for all of us as we tried to communicate in various languages. Eventually, the conversation turned to me: my vocation, what does a priest do, etc. The conversation wandered somewhere else in one of those unique international settings, people switching back and forth between French, Spanish, English, and German.

In the midst of the talking, this introspective French woman in her fifties blurted out to me, "Are you in full agreement with the pope?"—as if she could no longer control herself. The question was out of context, and an awkward silence fell over the table. Everyone glanced toward the two of us, and I gently replied, "I have great respect for the pope. Yes, I agree with him." Later that night, I showed her a copy of the book by Cardinal Ratzinger. She only looked at it but did not respond.

The next morning was the first official day of the Camino for me. I was out the door at 7:10 to climb over the Pyrenees, out of France and into Spain. My backpack with full water and food was just about twenty-eight pounds, with the American flag hanging off one shoulder and the Vatican flag hanging off the other. It is a fifteen-mile hike, rising to almost one mile in altitude, literally into the clouds. It was the moment of truth—after almost a year of preparation, can I really do this?

The first five miles were the steepest, and eventually, I arrived into the peaks of the Pyrenees. They were full of sharp drops and wafting clouds over the edges, drifting down beyond grazing sheep. They were some of the most moving landscapes to hike through. I eventually got a good pace going and climbed up into the clouds.

About two hours into the hike, I turned back to look back over Saint-Jean-Pied-de-Port, which was now deep in the valley below. The view was impressive, so I decided to stop and say my morning prayers. As I stood there reciting the Psalms, other pilgrims passed by me, and I became nervous that I was getting behind. I tried to calm myself, remembering that this was not a race, and reflected on that great lesson I learned in seminary: prayer is not time lost but time gained, and the Lord who is the Lord of time will work out the schedule according to His plan.

I met many people that first day who were also trying to conquer the mountains. I spent time walking up the green

El Camino de Santiago

mountainside with a young Danish man in his twenties whose mentor at work had done the Camino. He told me he had fallen in love with her, but she was not in love with him. He had been struggling with suicide, and so out of desperation in trying to find the spirit he found in his mentor, he decided to do the Camino himself. He was a sad young man who had trouble finding meaning in life. I shared some aspects of the Faith with him, but I wondered whether he would make the whole Camino.

Later, I passed a friendly couple from Finland in their fifties who asked me, "Do you have permission from the Vatican to wear that flag?"

I smiled and answered, "Yes, the pope asked me to do it."

Later, I walked with a kind Norwegian man in his fifties who had done the Camino many times. Now he helps pilgrims, especially getting over the Pyrenees Mountains. After discussing many issues, and why he has rejected the Catholic Faith, he told me every time he reaches Santiago, he receives Holy Communion. I told him he really should not receive Holy Communion until he believes what the Church believes. He replied, "Then most people would never receive Holy Communion!" Now there is something to ponder.

The two of us arrived at a deteriorating statue of St. Mary, which someone had placed on one of the rocky peaks, known by the pilgrims as Notre Dame de Orisson. I stopped and offered a prayer asking her guidance over the Pyrenees.

Just after noon, I reached the Spanish border and came to a sign that read "Navarra." I felt a great sense of excitement and triumph. Excitement because I was now entering the land of St. James and so many other great Spanish saints: St. Teresa of Avila, St. John of the Cross, and St. Ignatius of Loyola; triumph because I was making it over the Pyrenees, and throughout history, there were many conquering armies who passed over this passage into Spain, such as Charlemagne in the eighth century or Napoleon at the beginning of the nineteenth century. I knelt down, kissed the ground, and said a prayer.

By 3:00 p.m., I had reached Roncesvalles in Spain, thank God. The final entrance into Roncesvalles is all downhill, and I learned an important lesson that would stay with me for the rest of the Camino: after a day of walking, going downhill is much more difficult for the legs than going uphill.

I settled into the hostel (called an *albergue* in Spanish) that looked like it was made out of an old stone church, and the cavernous building was filled with over one hundred bunk beds. It did not really matter to me. I found a corner lower bunk and knew that I would sleep well that night. I then prepared for a pilgrim Mass the local parish was having that evening.

The parish was actually run by canons, priests who run a parish but live in community. What a Mass! I concelebrated the Mass with the five canons in this rather small but splendid thirteenth-century gothic structure. It had a huge organ with a young organist who knew just how to play it, and the acoustics were wonderful (no carpets!).

To my surprise, as we entered, we sang the *Asperges* in Latin (which we sing every Sunday at my parish for the Latin Mass) and the priest sprinkled the people with holy water. Then we sang the *Missa de Angelis* for the Mass parts (which we sing every Sunday at the ordinary Mass). It was great to be part of the universal Church—chanting Latin with my brother priests in a remote village halfway around the world. The beauty of the church with familiar Latin chants accompanied by an amazing organ was no small consolation to my weary body. At the end of Mass, the priest blessed all the pilgrims.

The next day, I passed through the charming village of Villava. I found the parish church, St. Andres, open, and a welcoming priest let me offer my Mass there. While setting up for Mass in the sacristy, we got into a cordial but very serious discussion. At the core of it was a disagreement about American politics, and the importance of working to end legalized abortion. It surprises me how Europeans have such strong opinions about American politics. I prayed for him and went on my way.

When I arrived in Pamplona. I went looking for the archdiocesan seminary with the hope of sleeping there, and when I knocked on the door, the rector graciously gave me a room. What a blessing. It was a wonderful break from the crowded hostels.

One learns a great deal about the local as well as the universal Church by visiting the local seminary. The clergy were mostly retired priests who prayed together and enjoyed good fraternity. I pray I can end my priesthood in the same way as these men: faithful and friendly to the end. I connected with a young Polish priest named Fr. Maruk studying at the University of Navarre. He allowed me to use his computer to write this column. Then I did a Holy Hour in the chapel—a satisfying Holy Hour, with so much to discuss with the Lord. I prayed for the various pilgrims I met, especially those who had helped me, and those who had left the Church.

Fr. Maruk then gave me a walking tour of Pamplona. The old city appears rather ominous and almost unclean. He brought me through the many historic churches. The most memorable landmark was the permanent memorial on one of the busy streets marking the spot where St. Ignatius of Loyola fell injured in battle, leading to his conversion. The archbishop of Pamplona was inspired to open a perpetual adoration chapel right there, hoping to bring others to conversion as well.

Now, after walking three days for a total of forty miles, my body feels relatively good. St. Francis of Assisi, with all of his body ailments, used to call his body "Brother Ass." Brother Ass can be stubborn, complain from time to time (feet, shoulders, knee), but ultimately goes where he needs to go. St. Francis also did the Camino during his life.

I have met people from all over the world—Spain, France, Italy, Germany, Austria, Holland, Denmark, Norway, Sweden, and even Japan and Australia. I had made the decision from the beginning to dress as a priest, wearing my Roman collar as a way of evangelizing on the Camino. It has borne some fruit in the many good conversations along the path. Almost everyone can either speak English, Spanish, or French; knowing Spanish and a little bit of French has gone a long way.

Travelling so openly as a priest on the Camino is like the parable, "The sower went out to sow his seed." I am simply walking into the vast marketplace of ideas in which we live today, and my mere presence is a proclamation of the gospel. Everyone immediately recognizes me as a priest, and the common bond as pilgrims gives us a familiarity. Inevitably, the question comes up, "So why are you doing the Camino?" People generally have a tendency to open up to a priest, and the Camino becomes an ideal place for people to discuss what is truly on their hearts. I often found myself simply listening to their stories as we quietly walked the Camino side by side. Marriage counseling is common along the Camino. When the opportunity arises, I bring the gospel into the conversation, helping them to see how Christ would view the situation; and, if he or she is Catholic, I sometimes hear a Confession.

Pope Benedict XVI, in his book *Introduction to Christianity*, spends a great deal of time discussing the idea of what it means to actually "believe" in the modern world. He writes that modern man has been conditioned to limit his view of reality, setting his heart on what can be measured, what is practical, and what is visible. The invisible world is beyond modern man's capacity in the sense he places no faith in it. Yet it is the invisible world which is more real and which, in fact, drives the visible world. How do you get modern man to open himself to this possibility?

This book, with all of its insights, has been particularly useful as I have had many discussions along the way with this vast array of people. Like so many of Pope Benedict's writings, he brings an insider's look into the European soul.

There are some practicing Catholics on the Camino, but the majority is no longer practicing, or non-Catholic. Nonetheless, there is a wonderful spirit among the people, and it seems many want to believe in something.

Already I have had an array of discussions—a French man who believes in reincarnation (isn't once enough?); a fallen-away Catholic who no longer believes because of the Crusades and the Inquisition (excuses); a Norwegian man who states the Gnostic gospels of St. Thomas and St. Mary Magdalene now disprove the Bible (no wonder Dan Brown's silly novels are so popular); a Spanish woman who says just being a good person is better than the hypocrites who go to Mass on Sunday (boring). Many a good discussion is the result, and I always finish by giving the person a blessed Miraculous Medal. However the conversation goes, the person is always very appreciative of the medal. Now Our Lady can make up for my poor efforts.

In the end, I am still wondering how to reach these people. On Monday night in Larrasoaña, the local church was locked, so I offered a Mass in the hostel for a group of ten pilgrims. Only one Italian woman received Holy Communion. The Gospel stated, "You see the speck in your brother's eye, but you do not see the plank in your own. Remove the plank in your own eye, and then you will see clearly how to remove the speck in your brother's eye." There was my answer. I will spend this next week pondering that passage.

Thank you for your prayers. I can feel them carrying me along, especially as everything goes so well. You are in my daily prayers as well.

Part 2: The Cross of the Camino, July 1, 2009

Fr. Markey hiking through the Navarre region up toward a local town.

It seems like an entire lifetime of events have happened since I last wrote, and the tone of the pilgrimage has dramatically changed. Perhaps it was an omen that I had a terrible nightmare here in Pamplona about Ernest Hemingway and his suicide. Before arriving at Pamplona, the Camino passes through the small town of Burgette, where Hemingway had lived and wrote for a period of his life. This whole area of the Camino is filled with markers referring to Hemingway. I have always found Hemingway compelling but dark, and his violent end only confirms that finding for me. That night in Pamplona, I had a nightmare about Hemingway that filled my being with utter nothingness, so much so that I had to get up and regain my composure. The tone of the Camino would now change.

On leaving Pamplona, I offered a Mass in the seminary for the feast of St. John the Baptist, hence got a late start, not getting on the road until 8:30 a.m. The Camino then passes through the internationally renowned University of Navarre, founded by St. Josemaria Escrivá. I suppose a priest praying the Rosary with a Vatican flag hanging off his back was not going to make it through this Catholic university without some conversations.

A professor of journalism, Dr. Jesús Tanco, immediately came up, and we began to walk and talk together. He was welcoming and quite the Camino enthusiast. Like the Emmaus story, the professor would not let me pass through without inviting me with my backpack into the campus buildings: he introduced me to many people, gave me a book on meditations on the Camino (more weight!), and then brought me down to the cafe and bought me a delicious *café con leche*. Finally, he called ahead to priests he knew on the Camino so I could stop at their churches as I passed through. By the time I finished receiving his warm hospitality, it was 10:00 a.m.—not a good starting time. The pilgrimage of penance was about to begin.

The day was already very hot, and the Camino led through some magnificent rolling wheat fields for miles and miles. I was having trouble getting a rhythm going, and Brother Ass was continually complaining. I finally reached the historic Alto de Perdón (Mountain Peak of Forgiveness) but found that it was hardly forgiving toward me. As I was descending, I turned my right ankle on a loose rock. I have a history of bad ankles from playing sports years ago, and I knew exactly what had happened. I ended up finishing the day once I got to the base in the small village of Urtega, having walked only nine miles.

Another issue was now arising: blisters. By the end of the week, more than a half dozen blisters formed on my feet. Everyone on the Camino gets blisters to one extent or another, and foot maintenance is a ritual for the pilgrims every night and morning. The common topic of conversation is, "How are your feet?" You learn more about your fellow pilgrim's feet before you learn about his or her life.

I then went out and bought cream to prevent blisters. Now, every day, I take out scissors, alcohol, and band-aids, tending to them, while at night, I let them air out. I also bought an ankle wrap for my swollen ankle. Seeing pilgrims limp along because of blisters or having a knee or ankle wrapped is not uncommon. Some pilgrims are amazingly strong and can do many more miles a day than I, while others have already given up and gone home. I have also passed two plaques dedicated to people who died at that spot on the Camino! May they rest in peace.

Brother Ass has been remarkably cooperative considering how much I am putting him through. When I arrive in the evenings, sometimes I can barely walk, and he tells me tomorrow will not be possible. When I slip out of my sleeping bag, he tries to discourage the day's journey and then spends the first mile of the morning's walk organizing a coup, enlisting mainly the feet and ankle but also anyone else who wants to complain. Nonetheless, once I get going, Brother Ass settles in for the day's walk. It is amazing that even with these feet problems, as long as the feet are kept straight and flat, they can go for many miles. I imagine this is how foot soldiers march for miles in their uncomfortable boots. This past Thursday, by the grace of God, I did my longest day of eighteen miles, trying to make up for lost time.

I met up with a delightful trio of Irish folk who did not know each other prior to the Camino but had formed a walking team. They first came upon me as I was praying my breviary beside the path of the Camino, and they asked if they could take my photo. After that, I travelled with them for a couple of days and had some of the best conversations of the trip so far.

One of these three Irishmen whom I find engaging is an economics professor named John, about fifty years old, who has travelled and taught in many places around the world; he has also written a number of books. John's brother-in-law just died, and he was trying to work through the grief here on the Camino. The two of us have spent hours during the Camino having serious debates over the Church, history, and current events.

John told me the Church in Ireland is being continually rocked by scandals, and because of the Church's historic role of influence in their country, the loss of its moral authority is being keenly felt. For the most part, it seems few are taking the Church seriously anymore. John concluded by saying, "The Church needs another reformer like Martin Luther to set things straight."

Confused by this statement, I answered, "The Church is always in need of renewal, but not with someone like Martin

El Camino de Santiago

Luther. He broke his priestly vows and married a nun! He was a deformer, not a reformer. Authentic reform comes from saints who are faithful to Christ and His Church, like St. Francis of Assisi and St. Catherine of Sienna."

After a bit of thought, John replied, "Perhaps you are right. I always liked St. Francis."

As an economist, John labeled himself a "Catholic Socialist," using his Catholic concern for the poor as a motive for large government programs around the world. He was concerned that the rich and the powerful were continually depriving the poor of a decent living. "It is true," I answered, "that the Church has always had a preference for the poor." I tried to explain to him the Catholic principle of subsidiarity, that the Church promotes localized personal responsibility. Large government programs can be dangerous because a powerful and intrusive government could possibly deprive the local community of its rights and responsibilities.

Like many Europeans I have met, John was passionately anti-President George W. Bush. John had spent time in the Middle East, taught in Tehran, and was convinced that the Iraqi War was motivated by greed and arrogance. John argued that his own experience along with various books he read supported this view. I simply asked questions trying to understand his position better.

Through this part of the conversation, I discovered that John had a skewed view of the United States. He thought the country was made up of dangerous gun-wielding Fundamentalist Protestants who had elected President

Bush to office, and John had trouble understanding how any Catholic could have supported President Bush. I explained, "Family/life issues are front and center for many Catholics in the United States, and this issue often defines how they will vote. To tell you the truth, Europe is far behind the United States in understanding the urgency of the pro-life issue. The right to life is the foundation for all other rights, such as the right to health care or education, so that without the right to life, all of these other rights become irrelevant."

"Yes, but what about capital punishment? President Bush was in favor of capital punishment."

"Opposition to capital punishment is not binding on the conscience of Catholics in the same way that abortion, euthanasia, or embryonic stem-cell research is," I told him. "Catholics are free to disagree over the application of capital punishment and still remain in good standing with the Church."

"Why?" he questioned. "It is all human life."

"Because the other issues have to do with innocent human life. Capital punishment has to do with those who have committed grave crimes."

"I do not accept that distinction!" John blurted out. Once again, my impression is that Europeans have strong opinions about American politics, but they fail to appreciate the importance of pro-life issues. That evening we put aside our differences and enjoyed a good dinner together. We continued to walk side by side the next couple of days, discussing religion, history, and politics, and I think we both learned quite a bit from one another.

As I continue to read the pope's book *Introduction to Christianity*, it forms a common theme for many of these conversations. He writes that the Church's attempt to bring about faith in the modern world is further hindered by the perception that the Church is a "garb of days gone by" and "a relic of the past." Today, the idea of tradition has been replaced by the idea of progress, and I sense this enthusiasm for progress in my discussions on the Camino.

Every two to six kilometers of winding paths through the hills and farmlands of Navarre, there is a charming medieval village of narrow, winding cobblestone streets and an elaborately carved church whose bell rings on the hour. While taken in by this, there is nonetheless a sense that this is a time gone by and no longer relevant to the modern world. Numerous times in my discussions, when I tell people I live about an hour from New York City, I hear, "Ah, the capital of the world!" America is the icon of progress, and so many yearn to go there. Trying to evangelize entails convincing others that the Church is relevant not only in these medieval villages we are passing through but in life in the modern world as well.

Giving out the Miraculous Medals is always rewarding. One Spanish woman who worked at a café in Lorca was telling me about her daughter who was involved in the parish youth group. She told me something I have heard quite often, "Yo soy católica, pero no soy practicante" (I am Catholic but not practicing).

When there was a pause in the conversation, I reached in my pocket and handed her the medal. "Es la Virgen," I gently said. She kissed it, and tears welled up in her eyes. She was so overwhelmed she had to walk away to control herself. Only the Lord knows what was going on in her life.

I talked with a young Spanish man who worked at a café in Sansol about the difficult economy and a bit about the Faith. At the end of our discussion, I reached in my pocket and gave him the medal. "Es la Virgen." He was surprised and clearly appreciated the gift. As I was leaving, he called me over and gave me a box of frozen pastries from the freezer for my backpack!

Every day, I have two goals: to find a church where I can offer Mass and to find a place to sleep. As I go through the villages, many times the parish church is closed. When it is not locked, I ask someone for permission to offer the Mass. I have brought a small Mass kit and vestments with me just in case.

On day six, I was passing through Irache, which is famous on the Camino because it has a fountain for the pilgrims not filled with water but with wine! The church there is a mammoth twelfth-century semi-gothic structure with two enormous cloisters. It was founded in the tenth century and filled with monks who tended to the pilgrims on the way to Santiago. There are no longer monks here today, and sadly, the huge structure is just an empty shell.

As I wandered through the cloisters, I found a door unlatched in the back—it led to the church! I went in and found the sanctuary quiet, dark, and cool—a wonderful break from the blazing Spanish sun. The church was completely empty, almost as though it had been forgotten for years. There, on one of the stone side altars dedicated to a saint I did not know,

I decided to offer Mass. I had candles in my bag, set them up, and had a most beautiful Mass by myself.

At the elevation of the chalice, when the Precious Blood of Christ was being offered, I prayed for the people on the Camino whose stories I had heard. I thought how ironic it is that the most powerful means of grace in their lives was being offered here in the silence of this old monastery, unknown to them. Though the times have changed, "Christ is the same yesterday, today, and forever." So much work needs to be done: "The harvest is rich but the laborers are few. Pray to the Harvest Master to send laborers."

The next day, I entered a village after a full day of walking and began looking for the local hostel. None of the hostels look the same, and some of them are in strange places. Perhaps it was because of the hot sun and the long day, but I wandered into a farmhouse where there were four scruffy men in their sixties sitting and talking. I asked them if this was the hostel; they laughed and replied, "No."

They saw my American flag, said some foul comments about the United States, and asked if I was an American doing the Camino. I answered, "Yes, thanks be to God."

One of them answered, "God? Bah! He has nothing to do with it." It was clear I was talking to nonbelievers.

After a few minutes of small talk, they asked if I wanted something to drink, to which I quickly answered, "Yes."

One sitting in a chair questioned, "Do you want water or wine? We know you priests like wine!" They all started to laugh.

It was harmless enough, and I laughed too. "I will take the water, thank you."

One of them brought me a tall glass of cold water, and I finished it. The refreshing water tasted great. I said to him, "Surely you will not lose your reward in Heaven for the water." They immediately stopped talking.

The one sitting in the chair intently looked at me and asked, "What do you mean?"

I answered, "Christ says in the Scriptures that anyone who gives even a glass of water to one of His disciples will not lose his reward in Heaven."

They then began to argue among themselves as to who would receive the reward: "Why does he get the reward? I helped too." I just sat back and watched. The face of the man who gave me the water changed. He suddenly looked bright and happy, like a child. Finally, they all were very helpful in directing me to the local hostel. I think the Lord wanted me to enter that farmhouse.

On the day I arrived in Viana, the professor from Pamplona had called ahead to the priest there and arranged for me to stay in the rectory. When I arrived, the priest welcomed me but told me he would not be available for a couple of hours. I decided to go to one of the side cafés for a pilgrim lunch.

While ordering, I noticed another pilgrim with a frosty cold mug of beer on his table. After a hot day on the Camino, the chilled beer looked just right. However, when I found out from the waiter how expensive a beer was, I declined. To my surprise, the pilgrim with the beer overheard the conversation, stopped the waiter, and said the beer was on him. Impressed by his kindness, I invited him over, and we began to talk.

He was a German biking pilgrim who had started his journey all the way in Germany. His brother had just died at the age of fifty-seven from cancer. Now he was doing the Camino in memory of him. We discussed many interesting topics, such as European history, World War II, and the Spanish Civil War, all over an ice-cold mug of beer.

At the end of lunch, he went for his bike, and I thanked him. He happily told me, "I have a beer every day for lunch on the Camino."

I felt like I needed a nap now and I wondered aloud, "How do you keep biking after a beer every day?"

Laughing, he said, "Each day after lunch I ride out of town, find a shady tree, and take a nap!"

A couple of days later, I was passing through the busy town of Najera and stopped at a church. The door was deceivingly modest, but the interior was a beautiful baroque masterpiece. The nave of the church was dark and empty, and I sat down in a back pew to pray in the quiet. I heard some shuffling behind me, and I noticed there was actually a sister in full habit behind a cloistered grill. I was in a Poor Clare monastery. I had not yet offered Mass that day, so I went over, introduced myself, and asked if I could offer Mass. She immediately opened up everything, got out the best vestments and chalice, called another sister, and I offered the Holy Sacrifice for the two of them.

The sister in her sixties then gave me a tour of the church. She told me St. Francis of Assisi passed through

Najera eight hundred years ago on his way to Santiago, and this convent sprang up after his visit. There were a number of marvelous statues of St. Francis in the church. Every time we came to a new one, she would stop in front of him, gaze at the image, and say with great affection in her voice, "Look! How poor and humble is St. Francis ... so unlike ourselves." She loves St. Francis. Afterward, she gave me a glass of orange juice and a hot tortilla/chorizo sandwich and sent me on my way.

When I arrived at the town of Azofra, they had the best albergue yet: two beds per room and a cold pool to soak your feet. My roommate, a young Spaniard named José, quickly told me, "No soy creyente" (I am not a believer). He was honest and friendly. I spent at least two hours soaking my feet in the cool water and it was the best they had felt all week.

Day ten was the low point of the Camino, but also, I would say, miraculous. As I was walking, the heat and blisters were sapping my energy. Many were passing me on the trail. I reached the town of Santo Domingo de Calzada, where one of the patron saints of the Camino is buried. I needed to go another four miles to reach the day's destination of Grañon, but I felt I could not take even one more step.

I stopped in the cool church of Santo Domingo de Calzada and simply sat in the pew. Although it was a historic church, they had unfortunately sanitized it of all emotion. It had "piped-in" music, a brightly lit reception center, and everything was polished to look more like a museum than a church. I found little consolation sitting in the pews because it felt more like a tourist center than a place of worship.

El Camino de Santiago

After spending twenty minutes in the pew and feeling no consolation, I approached the Blessed Sacrament chapel and prayed: "Lord, St. Paul says when we are weak, it is then we are strong. I feel very weak and not very strong." I then went and prayed at the tomb of Santo Domingo. Exhausted, I then visited a café for a soft drink and something to eat, but the refreshments were unappetizing. The television in the café was blaring loud images of promiscuity and rock music. Escaping, I headed back into the hot sun and, by the grace of God, pushed through the last four miles to Grañon. I slept for two hours on a simple floor mat when I arrived, drained both physically and emotionally.

At 7:00 that evening, there was a pilgrim Mass, and I concelebrated. The church, St. John the Baptist, was "just another" priceless masterpiece on the Camino: a stone gothic church with vaulted ceilings and magnificent multi-tiered baroque reredos carved in wood, gilded in gold, all filled with the various scenes from the life of Christ, Our Lady, and the saints painted in minute detail. So unlike the church of Santo Domingo de Calzada, this truly felt like a church. The choir loft was also unique in that it had choir stalls from when it used to serve as a monastery.

A young priest, Fr. Pachi, six years ordained, was very welcoming. It felt good to have a priest to talk with. Every fiber of my body ached, so I arranged with Fr. Pachi to spend the next day there in Grañon so my body could rest. However, I was now starting to get behind, and I feared that I may not make it to Santiago on time for his feast day.

Fr. Pachi asked me to read the Gospel at Mass. The Gospel was the story of Christ asleep in the boat while the waves crashed into the sides. When the disciples thought they were perishing, they awoke the Lord. The Spanish translation reads that the Lord said to them, "Cowards! Oh you of little faith." As I read this passage, I felt the Lord was rebuking me for my little faith, and I felt a glimmer of hope that perhaps I would reach Santiago after all.

The hostels usually do not feed the pilgrims, but this hostel in Grañon fed us a full meal: hot lentil soup with chorizo and a big fruit bowl for dessert. It was being run by a friendly American named Frank from Santa Barbara, California. I ate very well. The hostel was actually connected to the church, and we even had a "prayer service" in the choir loft afterward. I was asked to explain the church architecture to the pilgrims, and I finished by singing the Salve Regina, explaining that this was the last thing the monks did before they went to bed.

When the first rustling and zipping of the other pilgrims started the next morning, I could not sleep any longer, so I decided to arise as well. When getting dressed, I noticed that my feet were actually bearable. I organized my belongings and decided I would try to reach Santiago after all.

By the grace of God, I had an excellent day walking. For much of the day, I marched along with a young Canadian couple in their mid-twenties, Jared and Erika. We had met some days previously, but today was the first time we really talked at length.

Jared and Erika were both bright, having just finished graduate school with some kind of environmental conservation degree. Erika told me she practices yoga. They were living together, though unmarried, and hiking the Camino together before starting their careers. There were many young couples walking the Camino, living together, "sin verguenza." I, too, had worked on the political side of environmental issues before entering seminary, so we had a common background to discuss as we walked through the dusty hills of Navarre.

They were kind and obliging, asking me many questions about politics and the United States. Therefore, I ended up doing most of the talking. I noticed the further we progressed along the Camino, the more their questions became cautious. They probably recognized I was more socially conservative than they were. Neither of them appeared to have any religious background, and eventually, the questions became more personal, asking me about religion and my vocation.

Jared finally asked, "So why did you become a priest if you were working already?" I did not get the sense that either of them would be able to grasp the "gift and mystery" of a call to the priesthood, as Pope John Paul II called it, so I tried to explain it in more secular terms.

"I had been educated in the public school system my entire life, from kindergarten through the end of college. However, when I was graduating college, I realized that after all these years, the school system had failed to answer the basic but most important questions of life: Why am I here?

Why is there suffering in the world? What happens after death? These questions plagued me, as they do most people. I had been raised Catholic but never took the answers the Church was giving seriously. The Church seemed to me like an outdated institution, or at least that was what American culture and its school system taught. I began to examine many of the world religions, reading many books, and talking to people who had more knowledge in these areas than I did. I was looking for some answer beyond natural reason, believing that one of these religions must have the truth."

"Or none of them," Erika injected.

"I guess that is an option too," I answered, trying to be objective. "I personally found the writings of St. Augustine and St. Thomas Aquinas most compelling, recognizing that even if you are not Catholic, men like this are some of the greatest minds in the history of the world. Mother Teresa's example also spoke volumes to me. Over time, through prayer, study, and the good example of other Catholics, it became clear to me Catholicism was the Truth worth giving one's life for."

Their silence afterward left me thinking that although they were not ripe for conversion, I had nonetheless gotten them to consider what I was saying. Jared seemed to be more open to listening than Erika. For me, it was an energizing conversation and made me forget the continuous pain shooting through my feet.

By the end of the day, I had walked more than sixteen miles to Villafranca—miraculous, considering how I felt the previous day! The full meal, good conversation, and God's grace combined for optimum performance.

At the end of day eleven, I had walked 155 miles. Please continue to pray for me. I do not know what each day will bring, but I am counting on your prayers to carry me to Santiago. My daily prayers go to Heaven for the parish.

Part 3: The Grace of the Camino, July 8, 2009

I left Villafranca, and Brother Ass once again was not cooperating, especially when the first mile of the Camino path was climbing a steep mountainside. When I arrived at the top, I was greeted with a beautiful view. I found a happy young couple and their daughter warming some breakfast over a fire. Their inviting smiles encouraged me to approach, and they handed me a hot cup of coffee. They were from Estonia and spoke virtually no English, but we were communicating just fine. They were Catholic and happy to see a priest.

I faced an eight-mile walk to the next town of San Juan de Ortega, and my feet were full of blisters. While most people have two or three blisters, I had a dozen at this point. I had already switched out of my boots into sandals. Every step over the rocky terrain was painful and had to be measured carefully. I was considering that perhaps the Camino was coming to an end for me. I walked most of this part of the journey with some of the few Americans I have met, two ladies from Ohio. One of these ladies is a Spanish teacher, and we discussed Spanish history and language, which was a good distraction from my feet.

When we arrived at the sleepy village of San Juan de Ortega I was drawn to the church, and upon entering this small, stark gothic structure, I knelt down to pray. "Lord, have mercy on me, a sinner." Alone in the church, I read Matins and Lauds and felt renewed by the prayers. I returned to a café where many of my fellow travelers had already gathered.

As the day continued, I had to face climbing over the mountain peak Cruceiro. The climb was incredibly rocky, and Brother Ass was telling me he did not think he could do another three weeks of this. Doubts about finishing the Camino resurfaced. I had a long heart-to-heart conversation with the Lord, asking the age-old question, "Why am I suffering so much?"

And then I thought, "Why am I walking this Camino anyhow?" I was walking the Camino in honor of my ten years as a priest, and I was hoping this pilgrimage would be an opportunity to explore more closely Spain's rich Catholic history. I looked forward to being away from the normal responsibilities of parish life, praying in Spain's ancient churches, and peacefully walking through the hills of this beautiful country. I knew there would be sacrifices, and I would offer them up to thank God for the blessings of these years, in reparation for my many failures as a priest, and for the current intentions of my ministry. Still, this Camino had become more than I anticipated. For over a week now, the Camino had become more an hourly test of endurance than an inspiration, and I really did not know if I could complete the journey.

Reflecting deeper, I realized I also wanted the Camino to help me grow in faith. I wanted to purify my faith so being Catholic would be more than a club to which I belonged or a set of intellectual ideas to which I subscribed.

El Camino de Santiago

In his book *Introduction to Christianity*, Pope Benedict writes: "Christianity is not a system of knowledge but a way.... Christian belief offers truth as a way, and only by becoming a way has it become man's truth. Truth as mere perception, as a mere idea, remains bereft of force; it only becomes man's truth as a way which makes a claim on him, which he can and must tread." The Camino is this way.

How does this happen? Because on the Camino there are no pretenses, and the trail wears everyone down, even to the point of revealing our hidden faults. For example, the pope writes that the current climate in which we live has conditioned many of us to limit our ability for faith "for the most part unconsciously." How do we break through our strict self-reliance, the illusion that we are actually in control of our lives? He answers, "[Man] can only be liberated by allowing himself to be liberated, and by ceasing to try to rely on himself." If there is a powerful lesson on the Camino, it is that I am no longer in control; and just when I have no more strength and no more options, He catches me, reminding me He is ultimately in control.

When I arrived at the mountain peak Cruceiro, there was a tall cross about twenty-five feet tall made from two tree trunks supported by boulders. I walked a little further along the peak and sat down to do midday prayer. I looked west over the mountain and could see far off in the distance the historic city of Burgos. To visit the famous Cathedral of Burgos was one of the major hopes of this trip. After reciting the psalms, I peered out toward Burgos and felt a wonderful inspiration: go to have Mass in Burgos today!

This was no easy suggestion. I had already completed twelve miles today, and the destination village for the day, Cardeñuela, was at the base of the mountain about two miles beyond. I did not know how many more miles it was to Burgos, but at least another eight or ten. Nonetheless, I still had not offered Mass, and yesterday I had to offer Mass in the hostel, which is totally restrictive. Tonight, I would probably have to do the same in Cardeñuela, which was hard to bear. However, if I reached Burgos, I could offer the evening Mass in one of the most beautiful cathedrals in all of Europe! The sun was not too hot, there was a cool breeze, and, most importantly, my feet had stopped throbbing.

I then made a deal with Brother Ass: "If you get me to Burgos today, I will give you the day off tomorrow. No walking tomorrow." It was a deal. After so many hours of being horribly self-consumed, the thought of offering Mass in the Burgos cathedral tonight had changed everything. This moment was the most inspired I had felt on the Camino. I was joyful with the wind under my wings.

The time was approaching 1:00 p.m., so I climbed down the other side of the mountain toward Cardeñuela. When I arrived on more flat land, I continued on. I stopped for a snack at a café, told some of my fellow travelers my plans to reach Burgos, and set off. My walking companions for the last few days were staying there in the village.

Much of the trek to Burgos was on blazing hot pavement, which is cruel and damaging to the feet. Nonetheless, I pushed on—Mass in Burgos! I prayed many prayers out loud on the road—more Rosaries, Divine Mercy, the Jesus

Prayer, personal intentions, hymns. Although I was extremely tired, I felt the Lord close to me. I arrived at the outskirts of the city about 4:00 p.m. feeling hopeful. Regardless, the real work was about to begin.

Burgos is a large city, and like many large cities, its outskirts are spread far and wide. I thought I was close to the city's center, but I was not. I kept pressing on, but my feet were failing, and the busy city swirled around me. I stopped at a church dedicated to Our Lady and said a prayer before the Blessed Sacrament. By 5:30 p.m., a man told me I was still an hour from the cathedral. Unbelievable. Still, I pressed on—Mass in Burgos!

As I shuffled across the sunbaked sidewalk, a young Spanish man approached and asked if I needed help. I told him my goal: an evening Mass in the cathedral. He explained he had the afternoon free and would be happy to lead me there. I just stared at him: this man was an angel sent by God.

We walked slowly because slow was the only pace I could handle. He told me his name was Javier and he was named after the great Spanish saint—St. Francis Xavier. Javier was from Burgos and shared some of the interesting history of the city.

After some time, Javier told me of some painful family problems that had clearly done terrible damage to his life. There was physical and emotional abuse. Needing a break from the walk, I sat down on the bench of a busy street corner while he stood there in the midst of the rushing traffic and explained the entire story. Though my body was exhausted and thoroughly worn out, my tongue became as nimble as the pen of a scribe. I was able to dissect the entire tragedy with precision, its meaning in his life, and then pour healing balm all over the open wound. I had no strength, but God was speaking through me, and I could tell by his reaction that my words were having a profound impact, changing the way he understood the tragedy. It was an amazing conversation.

Finally, we arrived at the Burgos cathedral at 6:45 p.m. I asked the security guards if there was an evening Mass. One of them answered, "Yes, at 7:30." I made it! Mass at the cathedral in Burgos!

Javier told me he would now leave me. I turned to thank him and said, "I do not have much, but I give you what I have—a Miraculous Medal of the Virgin."

He warmly received it and said, "No, Padre. Es mucho" (No, Father, this is a lot).

I limped into the sacristy, and an older Spanish priest embraced me, receiving me like a father. I nearly cried when I told him the story: It was a miracle I was here for Mass. Of course, he could not fully understand what happened, but he was kind and gracious to me. We then offered Mass together.

The life-size crucifix in the sanctuary was clearly Spanish, with the most vivid signs of the bloody Passion covering the corpus. I noticed, in particular, Our Lord's black and blue feet, with a spiny nail ripping through the flesh. With my throbbing feet and having trouble even standing up for the Mass, I do not think I ever understood the suffering of Our Lord's crucified feet like I did at that moment. When I did my calculations, I had walked twenty-five miles that day.

Once again, I was asked to read the Gospel. It was the story of the paralytic, a man who could not walk, who was brought to Our Lord. Jesus told the man his sins were forgiven. Then Our Lord commanded the paralytic to get up and walk. The man got up and walked. Again, the Lord was talking to me. I felt liberated hearing those words.

The hostels do not allow pilgrims to spend more than a day in them, and you have to be out by 8:00 a.m. This was the only excuse I needed to secure a hotel room for two nights. The room was heaven, with a perfect view of the cathedral. I would spend the next day sleeping late, then touring Burgos. I slept wonderfully.

The priest from the night before was Don Ildefonso (named after a bishop saint from Toledo), about sixty years old, and a canon of the cathedral. "Don" is the Spanish title for a canon. Don Ildefonso, born in the outskirts of Burgos, was ordained for the archdiocese as a young man and had spent twenty years as rector of the local seminary. He was now the chancellor of the archdiocese of Burgos. He had worked hard for the Church; he understood the Church; he loved the Church; and most important, it was clear Don Ildefonso loved being a priest.

Don Ildefonso invited me to sing Lauds with the other canons and to have Mass at 10:00 the next morning in the cathedral. It was marvelous—about sixteen priests chanting, organ, and incense for the feast of St. Thomas the Apostle. An American priest was a novelty to the other clergy, and in the sacristy, they all wanted to talk to me.

Don Ildefonso gave me a personal tour of the cathedral. He called it "una poema de piedra," a poem in stone. The cathedral exceeded my expectations, filling me with the sense that those who built this church truly loved Christ. He was the center of their reality.

The Cathedral of St. Mary of Burgos.
Photo © Adrian Fletcher www.paradoxplace.com

Wherever we went, people were happy to see Don Ildefonso. This was his kingdom, and I was his privileged guest for the day. He invited me to lunch with the other priests—a full meal with local Spanish wine. When the day ended and I said good-bye, I felt inspired by the example of his priesthood. He had given his life to his archdiocese and would probably die there, hidden from the rest of the world, faithful and grateful to the end. How many priests are there in the history of the Church who have fulfilled their limited role in the Body of Christ, with no mention of them in the history books, yet faithful to the end? We will only know in Heaven.

This rest in Burgos was just what I needed, and I like to think my feet finally adjusted to the regular pounding of the Camino. I have now entered the Meseta, famous among the pilgrims for its long stretches of dry, flat land in the hot Castilian sun. The journey finally has developed into what I was hoping for: quiet walks early in the morning in the hills of Spain, saying my Rosary, grateful for the simple things in life. The churches in these towns are priceless works of devotion, and most people will never visit them, because they never travel to these parts of Spain. Perhaps I needed ten days or so of painful feet to soften my heart so I could truly appreciate every step as a gift.

By now, my Spanish was in prime form. Using the language every day, I would much rather speak Spanish than English, because I find it more playful and expressive. While one does not need Spanish to hike the Camino, speaking Spanish makes it a much richer experience.

Many more pilgrims entered the Camino in Burgos, especially young people in their twenties. I was now one of the seasoned Camino travelers, and I knew many people on the path. It felt good to be one of the veterans. After a few days, I witnessed new pilgrims limping, fluids oozing out of their feet. Lord, have mercy.

When we arrived at Hornillos on day thirteen, the hostel was noticeably more crowded. I met a young Irish couple who started in Burgos, and when the young man heard me speaking Spanish, he asked me to call him a taxi. When I inquired why, he told me after one day he had had enough and wanted to return to Ireland.

While people were washing up in the bathrooms, I overheard a number of the young people complaining about the "prudish" sex education programs of the United States, and how, unlike Europe, religion still influences the United States too much.

"Would that Christianity still had some influence in the United States," I thought to myself as I washed my clothes in the sink.

After cleaning up, I sat outside with some people from Scandinavia. There was a disproportionately high number of people from Norway, Sweden, and Finland on the Camino, and I always seemed to get along well with them. As we sat there writing in our journals and talking, the anti-religious people gathered at the table behind me. The discussion was led by a weathered Australian in his fifties eating tuna out of a can, surrounded by a couple of young Americans and Germans, who enthusiastically agreed to everything he was saying. They continued their talk, criticizing the United States' religiosity, such as placing God's name on our currency.

One of the ladies at my table asked, "Father, do you plan to go all the way to Santiago?"

I answered in a voice loud enough for the table behind me to hear, "Please God! Yes, I hope so." I could tell they heard me. There was then a stillness in their conversation and their negative discourse died down.

Later, I made my way into the parish church to pray. It was a smaller gothic church with a few of the typical Spanish baroque reredos. However, on the church's right side, there hung a large framed black-and-white photo of a young priest, from the chest up, in a cassock. He looked intelligent,

Seminarian Teodulo Gonzalez Fernandez of Hornillos: Martyr for the Faith, 1936.

disciplined, and serious. I immediately was taken by the photo. This young priest looked like someone who would have attended my seminary and who I would have befriended. Underneath the photo, it read: Teodulo Gonzalez Fernandez, Age 25, Martyr for the Faith, 1936.

In asking around, I learned Teodulo grew up in the town, entered seminary, and was killed in Madrid during the bloody Spanish Civil War (1936–1939). Most of what we hear of the Spanish Civil War in the United States comes from Ernest Hemingway or occasionally from the secular press, both of which are sympathetic to the Communist side, the Republicans. However, the Catholic Church sided with the Nationals. As with most civil wars, Spain's was brutal, with atrocities on both sides. With the Church siding with the Nationals, thousands of bishops, priests, and religious were dragged out into the streets by the Reds and shot, many of whom have now been canonized. Teodulo was one of these martyrs at the tender age of twenty-five. His family hung his photo up in the local parish church so he would not be forgotten.

The latent forces that inspired the anti-religious conversations earlier in the day are very much related to the photo of this young Spaniard. When this force reaches maturity, it leads to the death of men like Teodulo. I often sense this force growing stronger and stronger in our culture today, and the time of martyrdom in the West may soon be upon the Church again. For the rest of the Camino, I prayed for this group of anti-religious pilgrims and tried to reach out to them along the hardships of the path.

Later that night, I met the local priest of the town. He was nine years ordained. When I began to explain, "I am walking the Camino because I wanted to …," he interrupted me and quickly replied in that pointed manner in which Spaniards so often speak, "Oh, it is you who wanted to do the Camino? And not God who willed it?" The statement caught me off guard and I stood corrected.

On day fifteen, I arrived at Castojeriz, a long and narrow city built around the base of a mountain. It was Sunday, and I was able to concelebrate Mass at the large twelfth-century church around midday. The church was unkempt—so common among the small parishes in this region, probably because there is no resident priest assigned. Nonetheless, there are hidden treasures in the broken drawers and closets of the sacristy—old books, vessels, and vestments. In fact, in a set of old drawers, I found a fine gold and green fiddleback (classic Roman chasuble) under a pile of junk. I dusted it off, put it on, and waited for the visiting priest to arrive. He was an African priest from Burundi studying in Spain. He put on a mass-produced polyester chasuble. We must have looked like quite a pair concelebrating together. There were about fifty people present for Mass. The people were poorly formed, and the lack of order and reverence during Mass made the experience disappointing.

Afterward, I went to the hostel and met an intriguing Spaniard named Luis, about forty-five years old, who was doing the Camino in the reverse route, traveling back from Santiago. After walking to Santiago, Luis said his life had completely changed. Everything had become peaceful, and he felt loved by God. He commented, "The Camino is so good because God, Our Lady, and St. James keep providing for me day after day. So instead of ending my pilgrimage, I just turned around and started walking back." Luis also mentioned that he met a man who has been walking the Camino continually for seventeen years!

This city of Castrojeriz is famous for its role in the *Reconquista*, the reconquering of Spain, so it is worth reviewing a little history from this period. Muhammad died in roughly 630, and his disciples immediately began to conquer other lands. By the beginning of the eighth century, Muhammad's disciples had conquered the Holy Land, much of North Africa, and even parts of Spain. The Muslims eventually invaded most of Spain and were finally stopped in France by Charles Martel, the king of the Franks, at the Battle of Poitiers in 732. The Spaniards, inspired by Our Lady and Santiago Matamoros (St. James the Moorslayer), began the Reconquista in the north of Spain, trying to drive the Muslims out of Spain. King Ferdinand and Queen Isabella succeeded in driving the Muslims from Granada, the last stronghold, in 1492. Castrojeriz has a statue of Santiago Matamoros prominently displayed in its church in recognition of the Reconquista.

I mention this history because that evening, I was sitting in a quiet café by myself reading Cardinal Ratzinger's book when a young man approached me selling goods: watches, small electronics, etc. He was about eighteen years old. I politely told him I was not interested. Noticing his

El Camino de Santiago

disappointment, I put down my book and asked him how business was going. He told me business was slow. I asked him where he was from, and he told me Morocco. I told him I had visited there a number of years ago, and we discussed some of the features of his country.

He noticed the way I was dressed and must have thought I was reading the Bible. After a few minutes, he told me quite plainly about the Koran and that I should become Muslim. I told him I was Catholic and did not think Muhammad was a prophet. Our conversation on religion then proceeded: We covered prayer, the Koran, the claims of Christ, death, and judgment. He was standing above me as I sat in a chair—yet a great sense of peace came over me. I also explained what I thought were the inherent problems with Islam. His passion was getting the best of him, and he was often quoting the Koran to me in Arabic.

There was an unknown factor in this young Moroccan's zeal, but I still felt a great sense of peace. A Spanish woman who worked at the hostel was watching from a distance and her face showed concern with the intense nature of the conversation. Slowly, she started inching toward us, hoping perhaps that the young man would leave.

The young Moroccan and I continued our involved conversation. He told me that thousands of French were converting to Islam, which showed the truth of Islam. Finally, I had to tell him, "Look, Muhammad murdered other people in his life. Jesus was a man of peace. I will follow Jesus. Muhammad had many wives, including a nine-year-old girl. I will not follow him." Instead of deterring his zeal, my comment only further escalated the tension.

By this point, the Spanish woman from the hostel was standing next to me, and she calmly said something to divert the conversation. I followed her lead. She and I continued to talk for a few minutes; the young man just stood next to me, refusing to leave. Eventually, I turned to him and insisted, "Look, you are not going to convince me to become Muslim, and I am not going to convince you. I think it best for you to move on." The Spanish woman agreed with me. Outnumbered, he picked up his things and walked away, quoting the Koran to me in Arabic, even though I did not understand a word of it. After reflecting on the heated exchange, all I could say to myself was, "It is great being Catholic."

The next morning, the path out of Castrojeriz pushed up a steep hill for the first mile or so until it reached a plateau. There was a magnificent view overlooking the Meseta, and one could see the Camino path descend into miles of dry lands. Everything was just right, and I made a good pace over the arid ground.

On day seventeen, I left Fromista along the Rio Ucieza. The river was not that large, and it provided a beautiful walking path. I encountered my first large fields of sunflowers this day. In Spain, they call them "girasoles," or sunturners, because the head of the flower actually turns to face the sun all day long. The sea of sunflowers faces east in the morning toward the rising sun, and then as if by command, the entire field of tall sunflowers rotates until they are all facing west in the evening. The day was quiet, and I prayed my Rosary along the river as the vast sea of sunflowers rotated around me.

After some time, I noticed that the path had become tall grass, and I no longer saw the "flechas amarillas," the painted yellow arrows that direct pilgrims along the Camino. I saw a village in the distance and decided I better ask where I was. Like so many of these small towns, there was no one around. I finally found some construction workers. I approached one and said, "I am doing the Camino and I think I am lost." He looked right at me and said, "¡Seguramente¡" (That's for sure!). I was about two miles away from the Camino and had to walk back on the highway until I arrived at the city of Carrión de los Condes. It was the first time I had gotten lost, and I was actually grateful for the peaceful walking path I had taken alone.

I found an old convent of Poor Clares on the edge of town that was founded when St. Francis passed through the area eight hundred years ago. I introduced myself to the sisters. They all lived hidden lives within the cloister with full brown habits and white wimples wrapped around the base of their chins. I found that they had a room for me to spend the night, and I asked if I could offer Mass there. They agreed to have me offer the Holy Sacrifice for them at 7:00 p.m. that evening. This was perfect because it gave me time to clean up and relax.

I wandered through the small city, and it had a wonderful spirit. In the center plaza was a tall pillar with a statue of Our Lady on top. On the plaque below, it stated that the town had been consecrated to Our Lady, the Immaculate

Conception, in 1905, and then re-consecrated to the Immaculate Conception in 2005. The streets were filled with religious pictures and, unlike so many of these towns, seemed alive with people.

That evening, I went to the sacristy of the Poor Clares, and I could hear the sisters chanting Vespers. I found everything for Mass scrupulously laid out — pressed vestments, burse, veil, polished gold chalice with white hosts. These sisters loved the Holy Sacrifice of the Mass, and I felt at home.

At Communion time, I went to the grill to give these brides of Christ their Spouse, and each of them received Him on the tongue. Once each sister had received, she carefully passed the flat gold paten to the sister behind her. I was inspired to see that there were a number of young sisters in full habit. At the end, the Mother Superior received the Lord. Without saying a word, she looked at the paten, held it steady, and then handed it to me, looking me right in the eye. She was making sure that I understood that I needed to purify it of any Particles of the Host. I nodded to let her know that I understood. It is a great comfort to be with those who share the Faith.

On day eighteen, the Camino path split and the pilgrims had to decide which one they would take. The longer route went through the countryside while the more direct route stayed by the road. I noticed that most of the other pilgrims were going to take the more direct route. After a brief snack, I made my way for "the road less travelled" out into the fields.

Once I got my pace going, I realized no one had taken this route and there was no sign of civilization anywhere. At first, I was nervous, thinking that perhaps I might get lost out here all by myself. Nonetheless, the path was miles of exhilarating beauty that melted away any anxiety: a crisp blue sky, sharp tree formations, mountains dominating in the distance, and the fields were a flurry of blues and yellows scattered over the light brown earth. I felt a surge of gratitude for having chosen this route and imagined that the impressionists like Van Gogh or Monet must have been imbued with the same spirit when they painted fields such as these on their canvases.

I arrived at the village of Terradillos de Los Templarios, a town originally founded by the Knights Templars as a place to take care of the Camino pilgrims in the Middle Ages. The local church, St. Peter's, was a disgrace. Never had I seen a church sanctuary and sacristy so dirty. How awful and disturbing. I was able to offer a Mass with the permission of the local townspeople, but the disrespectful care of the house of God left me with a terrible feeling. I tried to clean both the sanctuary and sacristy as best I could before leaving.

On the edge of town, a well-dressed, middle-aged Spanish couple came up to talk with me. It took only a few minutes for me to realize they were Jehovah Witnesses. They were trying to convince me to join their church. I always admire how zealous the Jehovah Witnesses are—fearlessly trying to convert a Catholic priest! I knew that Jehovah Witnesses do not believe that Jesus Christ is God, but He is rather an angel, so I tried to convince them that Christ is God using Scripture. "The first chapter of Hebrews says, 'To what angel did God ever say, *You are my Son, today I have begotten You?*'"

When that failed, I tried the historical approach: "Don't you recognize how ironic this all is? The foundation of Christianity is here, in Europe, in Spain with St. James. Your new religion was founded in the United States, which broke away from Protestant churches. And now, you are bringing this American offspring of Protestantism back to Europe."

Or again, "I am an American. You are Spaniards. Don't you realize what treasures you are giving up by submitting to these American errors?" It was no use. In the end, we parted our ways, unconvinced.

I had now walked 250 miles—246 remained. So that day, I passed the halfway point. Thank God. While my feet looked much better, Brother Ass still had his share of things to complain about every day. I did not have any more Miraculous Medals. I shared fifty of them. Please know you are in my prayers, especially the sick, and I am counting on your prayers to get me to Santiago.

Part 4: The Rhythm of the Camino, July 19, 2009

I have not been able to write for the past week or so, because I have not had access to the internet. In many ways, it has been a blessing to be free from the computer.

The Gospel on Sunday, July 12, stated you should take very little with you for the "camino" (in Spanish), and you need to learn to trust in the Providence of the Almighty. The Camino of Santiago is, of course, a metaphor for life; perhaps that is one of the reasons so many people are drawn to walk these steps.

El Camino de Santiago

An important lesson on this Camino is learning to live simply and to rely on the Lord again and again throughout the journey. On the Camino, there is a rhythm, and we carry everything we need on our backs. The day is spent walking through fields, forests, and farms, and one really learns to appreciate the simple things in life. The changes in the temperature, the sunlight, and the terrain all make a big difference in the day. Some of the most satisfying moments are sitting in the shade eating fresh bread and the local cheese, cutting it with a pocketknife. In the evenings, you can taste the dry Castilian fields or the rugged Galician hills in a glass of the local wine.

One grows closer to his body, becoming sensitive to any and every pain, making sure the ailment is addressed. When we arrive at the hostels, we take a shower, and often there is no hot water. After cleaning up, we wash our clothes by hand in a sink or with a hose and then hang them on the clothesline to dry. We have to live in very close quarters with complete strangers, but everyone does a pretty good job of being courteous to one another. People are the same everywhere: everyone appreciates a little bit of patience and a little bit of charity.

After weeks of living like this, one starts to count on the goodness of God. He always provides the little things in life just when you need them. He is there at one's side whispering, "You see, I am right here, closer to you than you are to yourself."

After passing through the quiet, dry lands of the Meseta, I was heading to the city of León. The towns leading to León are poor and resemble the underdeveloped hills of Central America more than Europe. One afternoon, while walking through the fields, I met a shepherd caring for his sheep. He had three sheepdogs to help him herd and control about one hundred sheep. I greeted him in Spanish, "Hello! Are you the Good Shepherd?"

"Eh," he said with a smile and tilt of his hand back and forth, "more or less." He was an elderly man, and although he did not have many teeth, he had a pleasant smile.

"Do the sheep recognize your voice?" I asked him.

"Of course," he answered.

"And if I speak to them, will they recognize my voice?"

"No!" he quickly replied. We talked for a few minutes more—an innocent but satisfying conversation on this long, hot stretch.

I arrived at the charming town of Mansilla de las Mulas on day twenty and was able to concelebrate Mass with the pastor of the town church, Santa Maria. He was fifty-three years ordained a priest and appeared deeply faithful to his vocation. Like many elderly Spanish priests, he was right to the point with his words. We got along well. Before Mass, he exited the back of the sacristy into a dark room. There was a thick rope hanging from the ceiling of this room, and this elderly priest tugged hard on it. A ringing began in the church steeple. I had never rung the bell tower for Mass before, so I asked him if I could take a turn. He smiled and handed the end of the rope to me.

After Mass, I was eating dinner alone when I struck up a conversation with an energetic German couple at the table next to me. We discussed the similarities and differences between the United States and Europe and, in particular, how Europe is so much more provincial than the United States. People are far more protective of their own particular region in Europe than people are in the United States.

When we began to discuss the Catholic Church, the woman explained that people in Germany either leave the Catholic Church simply because they do not want to mark "Catholic" on their tax form "or because they can't stand the pope." Her cursory statement about Pope Benedict made me sad that the pope's own people would be so vehement in their rejection of him.

On July 11, day twenty-one, I arrived at León, one of the major cities on the Camino with an amazing cathedral. It was 11:50 a.m. and a handsome middle-aged couple walking by me shouted, "This way! They will celebrate the feast day Mass in honor of St. Benedict in ten minutes." I followed the people down the old streets of the city and came to a convent. Today was the feast of St. Benedict, the patron of Europe, and we arrived at the cloistered convent of the Benedictine Sisters of León. Out in front were about ten well-dressed men with folders practicing their singing. I asked them what they were doing. One of the singers showed me the Latin chant notation and explained, "We are the choir for the Mass, and we are going to be singing Gregorian chant."

I entered the sacristy and asked if I could concelebrate. Five elderly Spanish priests warmly welcomed me. I took off my backpack and prepared for Mass. In God's Providence, I had arrived just in time.

The Mass was a solemnity for the twenty Benedictine sisters in full habit. They sang beautifully along with the men's schola, and I was asked to read the Gospel. I offered my Mass for the conversion of Europe. Everything unfolded according to plan after the Mass. The sisters invited the other priests and I for a big lunch. One of the priests, Fr. Antonio, then offered me to stay in his priestly residence. The priests in Spain along the Camino have been wonderful to me the entire time. Everyone wanted to know who I was and why I was there.

These priests were all elderly, having spent their entire lives serving in the vineyard of the Lord. They knew each other well, and there was a quiet confidence in their conversation that can only come about through years of working together. The conversation turned to the Spanish Socialist prime minister José Luis Zapatero, who has fervently opposed the Catholic Church on many fronts. I did not realize it, but he was from León, and I was surprised when one of the priests told me that he had taught Zapatero in Catholic school when the prime minister was a boy. One of the other priests added that he knew his mother well and attended the funeral when she died a few years ago. He said she was a "beata," which I understood to mean she was a devout Catholic woman. I thought it strange that the prime minister would grow up in this atmosphere and end up so strongly opposed to the Catholic Church.

When the other priests and I were leaving, the Mother Superior caught me and said the sisters would like to speak to me, the "young American priest." In honor of the feast day, she invited me in to speak to them within the cloister. We entered the courtyard of the cloister, and all the sisters, about twenty of them, were sitting in a circle. The Mother Superior sat me down in the middle. They were joyful as they asked their questions: Why was I here? How did I receive my calling to become a priest? How did I know it was their feast day? My presence at the feast day was purely providential, and they were convinced St. Benedict brought me.

They also wanted to know my perceptions of the Church in Europe, what our new president, President Obama, was really like, and the state of the Church in the United States. Among other things, I told them that although the Church has its roots in Europe, and the Church in the United States has its share of particular problems, I think the Church is healthier in the United States in the sense there are more young people attending Mass and entering the priesthood and religious life. They were encouraged to hear this news because as one of the sisters noted, whatever happens in the United States will eventually have an effect in the rest of the world. They all had great love for Pope Benedict XVI, which solidified the trust in our conversation.

That night, I slept at the large priest residence where Fr. Antonio lived, and I was grateful to be out of the hostel for a night. Fr. Antonio had been ordained fifty-five years and always wore his cassock. This cassock was unusual because almost all the diocesan priests in Spain never wear even a Roman collar. Fr. Antonio reminded me of the famous brother St. Andre of Montreal. He did not say much, was hard of hearing, but in his own humble way, he was acutely attentive to those around him. The other priests generally liked Fr. Antonio, but I did hear one of them make a negative comment about his simple manner. Personally, I was proud to be Fr. Antonio's guest and walking through the streets with a priest in his cassock.

The next morning, I arose before sunrise and was surprised to find Fr. Antonio at the door in his cassock waiting for me with a smile. How long had he been waiting there? In the darkness of those early hours, he quietly led me through the winding streets of León to ensure I would not get lost finding my way back to the Camino. When he pointed me in the right direction, we said good-bye, and I started to walk away. However, something was not right. I turned back, ran up to Fr. Antonio, knelt down before him, and asked for his blessing. I was much the better man for having received it.

On Sunday night, July 12, I met a group of ten college students from the United States who started the Camino in León. They were part of the group FOCUS (Fellowship Of Catholic University Students). We kept coming across one another for the next couple of days, and eventually, in Astorga, we decided to travel together. I have now been traveling with them for about a week. These young people are a good example of why I am hopeful about the Catholic Church in the United States.

As I have learned, FOCUS is on college campuses around the country, and its purpose is to evangelize other

El Camino de Santiago

students, particularly through the study of the Bible. They are well-formed in the Faith; spending time with them has been a wonderful blessing for me on the Camino. Amazingly, most of them have had direct contact over the years, either in their home parish or on their college campuses, with my classmates from seminary. In some ways, the faith of these students is the fruit of the past ten years of my classmates' good work.

Every day we pray the Liturgy of the Hours and Rosary together, and I offer the Mass for them. They chant Latin very well! Furthermore, I have been engaging them in a number of talks and leading discussions on the Faith. I have become their "chaplain," to a certain extent, and have much enjoyed serving in this role. Their youthful joy and innocence are contagious. Yesterday, we picked up a seminarian from Michigan, so we are now a group of twelve traveling together, praying, and enjoying one another's company.

The day we left Astorga, the college students and I stopped in a village café for a tortilla. Many pilgrims were passing by, and a Swedish woman I knew approached with another woman in her fifties whom she had met and introduced us. She was an American from the Midwest and enthusiastically sat down next to me.

"I am a priest also, in the Episcopalian Church." Not sure what to say, I nodded in acknowledgment.

Pointing to my Roman collar, she continued, "I could not wear my collar because people over here would not understand."

"I think you are right," I answered. The college students listened intently to the conversation.

She quickly went on to explain how disappointed she was that the priests here in Spain, beginning all the way back in Roncesvalles, would not give her Holy Communion at Mass. I am not sure, but I think she thought that a priest leading a group of young American college students might be sympathetic toward her feminist agenda. I asked her why she would be surprised, as this was the teaching of the Catholic Church.

Aware that I was not sympathetic to her predicament, she replied, "I was hoping that the Church would be more inclusive here."

"The Church is very inclusive," I answered. "If you want to receive Holy Communion, all you have to do is become Catholic." Upset with my reply, she turned away and did not want to talk anymore.

To her surprise, the college students were not supportive either. They could see there was something wrong in her approach: as a leader in her church, she was guiding people even further away from the apostolic Tradition and then attacking the Catholic Church for being so closely identified with it. All this while, we were walking toward the tomb of one of the apostles! Later, my new college friends and I discussed the fact the Anglican Church is being torn apart by attitudes such as this woman's.

As for Brother Ass, many nights he still complains, making me sometimes wonder how I am going to get up tomorrow and walk another day. I now have a brace on my left knee as well. However, after twenty-nine days of walking, I am confident when I awake the next morning and hit the Camino before the sun rises, Brother Ass will perform as needed. Ultimately, he has been faithful to his master, and I am praying he holds out these final days.

That afternoon, we arrived at the village of Rabanal where we found a small but comfortable hostel named *Nuestra Señora del Pilar*. I went through the normal routine of a shower, putting on the one set of clean clothes, and then hand-washing my dirty clothes with the hose. There was an elderly Spanish woman who worked at the hostel, and she was watching me hobble around with my bruised feet. As I hung up my clothes on the clothesline, she said that I needed to soak and massage my feet because they did not look good. She offered to do it for me, but I politely declined her offer.

That evening, the college students and I had Mass in the small local church. It was the feast of the Native American Saint Kateri Tekakwitha, and I preached on how much she suffered before she died when she was just twenty-four years old. After dinner, I returned to the hostel, and the elderly Spanish woman once again saw me hobbling around. For a second time, she insisted on attending to my feet. This time, I gave in and allowed her motherly instincts to take over.

She took my feet and soaked them in warm water and salt. Afterward, this kind woman took them out, dried them, and began to massage them with a cream. She said that my feet were swollen, and after looking at all the dried blisters, she asked, "How did you endure all of this?" It felt good to have someone recognize what I was going through.

All I could answer was, "God is good."

Because I was wearing my Roman collar, I wondered with all the people wandering about if it was scandalous to have a priest attended to this way by a woman. Afterward, I reflected that Jesus also allowed a woman to publicly anoint His feet with ointment and even to kiss them and that the people of His time were scandalized.

On July 15, day twenty-five, we left Rabanal at 6:20 a.m. It was cold, windy, and dark. We prayed the Rosary huddled together like sheep climbing up a mountain, trusting that the warm light of the sun would eventually come. As the sun rose over the mountains, so did another enjoyable day.

We arrived nineteen miles later in Ponferrada at a very large and busy hostel, with hundreds of bunk beds. I knew many of the pilgrims there, and I enjoyed catching up with them. I wanted to rest, but the students were hungry, so we went to dinner at a simple outdoor café in the local plaza. We ordered the bargain pilgrim meal, which was common in most towns: soup or salad, the main dish of pasta and meat, dessert or fruit, and a bottle of water and wine; all for nine euros.

It was a joyful dinner, and while we innocently talked about the day, I noticed a young man on a doorstep not too far from our table. I think he was a Peruvian Native with dark brown eyes and long straight, dark hair, about seventeen years old. His face lacked emotion and his eyes were intently fixed on our group. From our position, I was the only one who could clearly see him; after a few minutes, I started to become alarmed. Purposely, I looked directly at him, hoping he would turn away, but he continued to stare. Something was not right here. I was relieved when he eventually got up and walked away across the plaza.

After dinner, I went into the beautiful church at the end of the plaza to pray by myself. There was an image of the Blessed Virgin at the entrance with the words inscribed in Spanish: "Let no one pass this way without imploring Our Lady's assistance." The church was quiet, dark, and beautiful—just right for prayer.

Blending in anonymously with the darkness of the back pews in this large stone church, I was able to encounter the peace of the Lord. It was as if I simply disappeared into His presence. Suddenly, the thought hit me that in a little more than a week's time, I would be back in the parish with the full weight and pressure of being a busy pastor on my shoulders. Of course, this is what the Lord is asking of me, and I must do it, but the thought of leaving this ancient pilgrimage and returning to full responsibility of parish life caused me some hesitation as I left the church.

On my way back to the hostel, I got lost in the narrow stone streets. In my confusion, I passed a quiet alleyway and was startled to see the Peruvian young man again sitting alone on a doorstep with that same blank stare! What was he doing here? Again, something was not right, but this time I felt sorry for him. God was present in this young man, and he looked terribly alone. It pained me, but what could I do? At that point, I just said a prayer and kept going until I found my way back to the hostel.

As I walked, I thought to myself, "Perhaps he was saying to himself, 'Why am I here half around the world away from my native country? Why don't I have friends like they do? Why don't I have food at restaurants like they do? Why don't I have the things they have?'"

Then I realized how blessed I am to be a Catholic priest, with Catholic friends; to have a vocation as the pastor of a busy parish, however challenging I may find it. Doing God's will is the most important thing in one's life—even more important than serving the poor—because if everyone did God's will, the poor would be served. God knows how to serve and save everyone, if only more people would do His will. When I arrived at the hostel, I finished praying my breviary and went to bed.

On day twenty-seven, Brother Ass was not looking forward to the walk. This day we were going to climb the steepest part of the Camino up to Ocebreiro. The walk on flat land lasted for nine miles, and then with no time for transition, the Camino shot straight up a five-mile track through primitive mountainside villages where we had to share the narrow path with migrating cattle and sheep. Rather than tiring me out, however, the challenge of the climb was exhilarating. Only the Lord knows why sometimes on the Camino I feel terrible and other times I feel good.

Ocebreiro is a small mountain peak village that seems as if time has stopped. There is not much more to Ocebreiro than some ancient stone buildings and cobblestone streets, with a ninth-century church devoted to Santa María. The view was spectacular, and it was hard to believe we had walked all the way up. However, we were like the Holy Family because there was no room for us at the inn. The small hostel was already full and there was nowhere for us to go this late in the afternoon. What made it even worse was the cold wind whipping around. The locals told us that such cold weather was unusual this time of year. We ended up negotiating our way into a local "meson," where we packed into a few rooms.

When I went looking for the rest of the college students, I found one of the young ladies from our group behind a rock wall crying alone. She had had a bad knee for days. Today's steep climb along with nowhere to stay on this cold mountain peak was all too much. After a little encouragement, we got her to her room.

Ocebreiro is known for a Eucharistic miracle inside the church of Santa Maria. In the fourteenth century, a peasant hiked up the mountain to attend Mass during a snowstorm. The local monk was dismissive of this peasant showing up during the storm but agreed to offer the scheduled Mass. The peasant's faith was rewarded when the bread and wine physically turned to flesh and blood during Mass, with just the two of them present. The miracle was approved by the Church and is now preserved in a gold reliquary donated by King Ferdinand and Queen Isabella.

When the priest in Santa María heard that I could speak Spanish, he asked if I wanted to take the evening Mass. I quickly answered yes. This was a great blessing, reminding me of what the sacred hands of a priest are meant to do — change the bread and wine into the Body and Blood of Jesus.

The next day's walk out of Ocebreiro to Samos was magnificent. On the hilltops of Galicia, one can see for miles over hilly farmland. We strolled into valleys, along rivers, and through green forests. It was also Saturday. Strangely, in Spain, the churches do not offer Saturday morning Mass anywhere. They only offer the Saturday evening anticipatory Mass for Sunday. This meant that today I had to look for a church where they would allow me to offer Holy Mass.

By midafternoon, it became clear that the few churches along the way were closed and we would have to offer Mass outside. It was a beautiful sunny day, and tucked under some high trees, to the left of the Camino path, we found a rock wall that could act as the perfect altar. Beyond the rock wall, the land gently sloped down to a flowing river below. I took out my vestments and chalice from my backpack and laid them out on the wall. Putting on my vestments, we all faced the rock altar overlooking the river, and I then began Holy Mass.

All was quiet. The sunlight was bristling through the leaves, the birds were singing, and the sound of the river trickling gave a rich background. At the moment of consecration, the Creator of this natural cathedral humbly descended on the rock wall. A great stillness enveloped us.

I could hear a couple approaching along the path, and instead of passing by, they stopped, took off their backpacks, and watched us from a little distance away. Everyone in our group was kneeling on the ground close to the rock altar. The couple watched as I slowly walked over and placed Jesus on each of their tongues.

Fr. Markey offering Mass on the Camino with FOCUS missionaries.

When Holy Mass was over, the stillness was so rich that no one dared to break it for about three or four minutes. Even the mysterious visiting couple stayed silent. They simply put their backpacks over their shoulders and continued walking past us, holding hands, without even saying a word.

Today is Sunday, July 19, and I am in the city of Sarria, about one hundred kilometers (sixty-two miles) from the goal of Santiago. I talked to my parents on the phone here, and it was a great consolation to me. Please God, I should arrive on Friday, July 24, the day before the feast day of St. James. On Saturday, July 25, I hope to concelebrate the Mass at St. James's tomb with the archbishop of Santiago.

The experience of the Camino has been exhausting—perhaps the most physically demanding thing I have ever done in my life—yet filled with many graces. The Camino beats you down, wears you out, and purifies you. At a minimum, it has shown me that I am able to endure much more than I expected. With God's grace, we actually can handle more than we realize.

I am also unsure of any other experience where you can meet and immediately bond with so many different people from around the world. More than ever, the Faith seems like "the universal message of salvation" that must be preached to the nations. The world may be smaller, but the message is even larger. Virtue applies to all, no matter where one is from.

When I arrive at the tomb of St. James, I will be praying for the families of St. Mary Church and all the special intentions people have given me.

Part 5: The Fulfillment of the Camino, July 28, 2010

During my final week of the Camino, I continued travelling with the group of Catholic college students, FOCUS. There was levity to these final days. As a group, we had become very comfortable with one another. In addition, Brother Ass was behaving himself. He complained little, particularly because he could now see the end was in sight.

Often in the evenings, one of the students would give a "witness talk" to the group, explaining why he or she is practicing the Catholic Faith. I have now heard almost all of them, and each is quite inspiring. Some have always been practicing and, as young adults, embraced the Faith even stronger, while others are converts, having to make large sacrifices to be Catholic. A few are the children of baby boomers, and their parents had left the Catholic

Church many years ago. However, the baby boomer parents are struggling to understand why their children are now becoming Catholics. In fact, in the stories I heard, the student's decision to become Catholic is causing real tension in the family.

The Faith was a constant topic of conversation when we walked, and while they regularly ask me to explain certain parts of the Faith to them, I thoroughly enjoyed hearing their experiences and perceptions. I was not sure why, but for days they had been asking me to talk about the Church's view on contraception. They all had some basic understanding of the teaching, but they wanted more details. One evening in Palas de Rei, we had some quiet moments in a plaza together to have the discussion.

I explained how contraception not only violates the natural law by eliminating the procreative purpose of the conjugal act but also turns an act that is meant to give love into an act of selfishness, using one's spouse as an object of pleasure. They were all very attentive. For this reason, contraception leads to increased selfishness in marriage and even divorce. I also noted that rather than contraception preventing abortion, it only increases abortion because people seek another option once the contraceptives fail. In the discussion, a few of the young ladies already had impressive medical knowledge of Natural Family Planning. They were convinced contraceptives are one of the most destructive forces in the world today. No wonder their baby boomer parents are getting upset!

For thirty-one days, there had been no rain on the Camino, most days sunny and dry. There were only three days left for the Camino, and I was convinced that I would not have to use the rain gear I had brought. However, here in Palas de Rei, I was woken up early in the morning by a terrible rainstorm. This storm was a foreshadowing of what was to come. Galicia, this final region of the Camino, is mountainous and green and known for its stormy weather. I would now experience the heavy rains firsthand.

The college students and I left at 7:20 that morning, and although dry outside, the sky was foreboding. As we did every morning, we started the walk by praying the Rosary together. By the time we had finished, the rain had begun. It never stopped. Even an hour and a half later, we were enduring a continual and total downpour.

Nonetheless, there was something energizing about this new experience. There was little talking among the pilgrims in the midst of the heavy rain as the Camino's path weaved through the rolling hills of Galicia. The thick rain falling on the leaves of the trees, the heavy mist in the distance, and the silence among the people made for a peaceful journey. The Lord was now fertilizing the many seeds planted during these past thirty days of the Camino.

We stopped for lunch in Melide, the *"pulpo capital del mundo." Pulpo* is cooked octopus, and Galicia is famous for its good *pulpo*. The restaurant was remarkably accommodating to all the wet pilgrims, and we feasted on an enormous lunch. I had tried pulpo a couple times previously in the United States, but this pulpo, diced and seasoned, tasted much better than I remembered—especially when wet and tired.

At the start of the next day, most of us still had damp clothes, but at least it was not raining. However, by the end of the morning Rosary, the rain began falling hard again. The downpour continued the rest of the day.

On day thirty-four, July 24, the final day of the Camino, I could not wait to get up. After trekking almost five hundred miles, it was hard to believe that today I would arrive. Santiago de Compostela was just twelve short miles away. I felt like a child on Christmas morning, excited to get out of bed. Brother Ass was rejoicing that he could finally take a rest at the end of the day and would not be subject to another day of long hikes. Furthermore, after so many hardships, and when at times I truly did not know whether I would finish, the journey would now be fulfilled.

When I went to put on my ankle brace, it broke, but I took it as a good sign. I hit the path and walked at a quick pace this day. The excitement made any remaining complaints of Brother Ass virtually nonexistent. The rain came once again, but it no longer mattered. I was going to be in Santiago in just a few hours.

When we arrived at the outskirts of Santiago, the rain stopped; by the time we came close to the center of the city, providentially, the sun started to break through the clouds. To see the spires of the medieval cathedral in the distance was immensely satisfying. Just before we entered the main plaza at 11:15 a.m., the students and I began to sing the *Salve Regina* in full voice. As we reached the center of the plaza, an Italian television crew caught sight of us and came close to film us singing together. We turned to the cathedral at the center of the plaza and prayed three Glory Bes, giving thanks to the Most Holy Trinity. I then gave the students my blessing. We all felt great relief for having made it and gave a loud cheer.

After taking photos, we made our way into the Santiago cathedral for the noon Mass. The Mass was packed with pilgrims, and I concelebrated at the main altar, above the tomb of St. James the Apostle. The Camino was over, and I had made it — *Deo gratias.*

A Spanish priest working in the United States had contacted friends of his in Santiago on my behalf, and they were expecting me. I was well taken care of and ended up staying in the apartment of the chancellor of the Archdiocese of Santiago, Don Elisardo Temperán Villaverde. I had not shaved for more than a month and was able to shave off my beard in his apartment. Don Elisardo went out of his way to make me comfortable. He also had a fascinating library of Spanish history books in his apartment from which I had trouble pulling away.

One of the rewarding parts of walking through the busy streets of Santiago during these next few days was meeting so many of the pilgrims I had met along the Camino. A number of them took the Miraculous Medal that I had given them out of their pocket to show me they were still carrying it.

The most remarkable encounter was with a Canadian woman in her early fifties named Jill. About three weeks ago, I had spent a few days, on and off, walking with Jill and her boyfriend, Gerald. He was also from Canada. The two were raised Catholic, divorced, and now living together, along with their kids from their marriages. They were a gentle couple, and I could tell they were happy to have the opportunity to spend so much time with a priest. The three of us spent long parts of those days enjoying one another's company on the Camino, even having a couple of meals together.

Inevitably, the subject of their divorces came up, and we discussed each of their separations in depth. My heart was pained by the terrible details. With similar backgrounds, they had found each other and were now trying to build a new life together. They had decided to do the Camino to help form a deeper bond.

The long hours of conversation along the Camino had built trust between us, and during the second evening of dinner, I found the right opportunity to say what I needed to say: this new bond between them was not pleasing to God.

"As painful as those divorces were, you are still married. The happiness that you want is not going to be found in breaking God's laws."

It was a conversation among friends, and there were no hard feelings. We discussed some options on how they could move forward, such as the Church's annulment process. The next day, we drifted apart. I have not seen them since.

On this day in Compostela, I ran into Jill on one of the small side streets. We were joyfully surprised to see one another, and she proudly showed me the Miraculous Medal I had given her.

I asked her where Gerald was, and she replied, "Father, he and I separated about a week ago, and I have not seen him since. I do not know where he is. We talked a lot about what you said, and we decided that it was best to separate and finish the Camino on our own. We are now going to go our separate ways." When I first met them, I could see a goodness in each of them, and now my respect for them grew even more. Jill and I traded a few more stories and then we parted ways.

A most friendly priest led me around Santiago during these few days from Opus Dei, Fr. José María Santana. I have no formal connections with Opus Dei, but I have always been impressed by their charity and their formation. Fr. José María was a great model of these virtues. He spent the next few days introducing me to his friends and taking me to the most important sights of Santiago.

That evening, there was Solemn Vespers in Latin led by the archbishop of Santiago, Julián Barrio, and a professional choir. They chanted the twelfth-century antiphons of St. James from the mysterious *Codex Calixtinus*, and their polyphonic neumes filled the church—truly magnificent.

At 11:30 p.m. in the main square, the city officials presented a fireworks/multimedia display on the façade of the cathedral before thousands of people, which was unlike anything I had ever witnessed. I was filled with gratitude to be there.

The next day was Saturday, July 25, the feast of St. James. It had been my goal to arrive for this day, and by the grace of God, I was here. The day before, one of the priests told me I should not plan to concelebrate the Mass with the archbishop on the feast of St. James because it was by invitation only. His comment troubled me, but I would at least try.

When I arrived at the sacristy of the cathedral the next morning, it was filled with many official-looking people

El Camino de Santiago

walking around, and everyone was in a rush. I walked up to the woman at the desk and asked, "May I concelebrate the Mass?"

She was clearly busy and answered, "Only if you are on the list."

"Can you please check?"

When I gave her my name, she went down the list and found "Fr. Greg Markey, Connecticut, USA." Surprised and relieved, I simply asked her where I should go to vest.

"To the library."

I walked across the outdoor courtyard and tried to enter the library, but there were security guards there. I explained to them that I was one of the priests for the Mass. Without much hassle, they let me through and led me into the back room of a small but magnificent library. The ceiling was a baroque fresco, and the room contained many priceless manuscripts under glass. The room was filled with about fifteen priests from various countries and five bishops. I was pleased to see Fr. José María there as well. He made it a point of introducing me to most of the other priests in the room, including Fr. Raniero Cantalamessa, the papal preacher who was visiting from Rome, and Archbishop Barrio of Santiago. To be among these distinguished clergy was a grace, and I thought it best not to ask how my name got on the list. I was simply grateful to be there. Everyone's vestments were meticulously laid out around the room with name cards on top of each folded chasuble. I found my set and vested for the Mass.

The procession of clergy wound around the outside of the cathedral through the various plazas with a precious relic of St. James carried on silver-gilded float. When the procession arrived in the main plaza, we were greeted by a military orchestra and infantry shooting their guns. At the head of the soldiers were various government officials. There is an ancient tradition that the king of Spain would be present for the feast of St. James, but now he only comes when the feast falls on a Sunday. This day, the king sent a representative: Alberto Núñez Feijóo, the president of Galicia.

The procession stopped in front of the soldiers so that the archbishop could greet the president. I found this warm greeting between Archbishop Barrio and President Núñez quite ironic. With Spain becoming increasingly secularized, the ancient religious traditions are nonetheless too deeply rooted in their culture to be ignored. Even the secular public officials must recognize the Catholic saint who brought the Faith to their land.

We processed into a packed cathedral, leaving the military band outside and entering into sacred hymns played by the organ. While the whole Mass was memorable, two things stood out. The first is a tradition that the king would address the archbishop within Mass about what the nation of Spain needs from the Catholic Church. This is unusual because a layperson is normally not permitted to preach during Mass. Since the king was not there, President Núñez gave the address.

In his elegant Spanish, he gave a compelling talk about various social needs, such as helping immigrants and the outcast. I was impressed that he quoted Pope Benedict XVI numerous times. President Núñez boldly proclaimed, "Just because a nation is technologically advanced does not mean it is morally advanced."

"Yes," I thought to myself, "we have become blinded by a false sense of progress." He finished by giving a lengthy and moving petition, imploring St. James's protection over the entire country of Spain. I imagined he must be Catholic to speak so passionately about St. James.

The archbishop, speaking as a "successor to the apostles," was then given an opportunity to answer the king's representative about how the Church could help the country. He asserted that Spain is suffering from an "immoral anthropology" in the sense that God is no longer part of the culture, and in losing sight of God, Spain no longer understands what it means to be human. He concluded by asserting, "The Church does not seek to impose anything. It

Archbishop Julián Barrio Barrio preaching on the Feast of Santiago, July 25, 2009. The President of Galicia, Alberto Núñez Feijóo, on the left, sits listening. Fr. Markey sits among the priests, second from the right.

only proposes a defense of the family and human life." I thought this statement could equally apply to any country in the Western World.

The second memorable part of the Mass was at the end when the cathedral servers swung the famous *Botafumeiro*, the world's largest censer. The archbishop placed incense on the hot burning coals, and a group of about six men swung the large metal container, sending it over the people's heads at lightning speed. Traditionally, the ascending incense represents the people's prayers going up to Heaven. The local people proudly sang a hymn they knew by heart. While impressed at this cultural icon swinging back and forth, the American pastor in me thought about how this censer could be a huge legal liability. I tried to put this idea out of my mind and simply enjoy St. James's feast like the rest of the pilgrims.

Archbishop Julián Barrio Barrio fills the famous botafumeiro, the world's largest thurible, for the Feast Day.

On Sunday, I was blessed with the opportunity to offer a private Mass on the tomb of St. James. The altar containing the precious relics is a small cavern underneath the high altar that the security guard had to unlock. There before me, in this intimate space, were the bones of St. James the Apostle. I offered a Latin Mass for the intentions of my parish, particularly those who asked for special intentions. The college group joined me for one last time, standing just outside the altar area, and we felt privileged to spend these final moments so close to Santiago. Afterward, we had breakfast together and then said our tearful goodbyes.

With all of the activities, I had almost forgotten to turn in my *credencial*, my pilgrim passport full of stamps from all the towns. I made my way over to the pilgrims' center, presented my *credencial*, and received the official *Compostela*, the certificate verifying the completion of the 496-mile journey. The certificate, in Latin, reads:

> In order to make ready at hand for all the Faithful and Pilgrims coming together from the whole world, either because of a desire for devotion or because of a vow, a document authenticating visitation to the shrine of the apostle, Saint James, patron and protector of the Spanish people, the Chapter of this beneficent Apostolic and Metropolitan Church of Compostela, which is the custodian of the seal of the Altar of Blessed James the Apostle, presents to all and to each who will examine this

document, and makes note: *Dominum Gregorium Markey* has visited this most holy Temple with piety because of his devotion. In the faith of those presenting this document, and strengthened by the seal of this Holy Church, I confer this document upon him.

Given at Compostela this 26th day of the month of July in the year of the Lord 2009.

In the afternoon, Fr. José Maria invited me to lunch at one of the Opus Dei centers in Santiago with a distinguished group of about thirty Spanish priests, professors, doctors, and journalists. At the end of lunch, I was surprised to find that I was asked to give a talk about my experiences on the Camino to the group. I was nervous when I stood up to speak, fearing that among these Spanish intellectuals, my Spanish would not be good enough. Once I began to speak, however, I became more comfortable in expressing my thoughts, especially after they responded with a few hearty laughs to some of my stories. In fact, being able to share my Camino experience with this illustrious group made for a satisfying exchange.

Later in the day, Fr. José Maria drove me to the city of Finisterre ("the end of the earth") and along the beautiful coast of Galicia. Poetically, the soft sun setting over the water to the west was the sign that my sabbatical was coming to an end.

As I flew out of the airport in Santiago the next day, I reflected on Pope Benedict's point in *Introduction to Christianity* that man experiences God not only in the poverty of human existence but also in the fullness of human existence: "Where men have experienced existence in its fullness, its wealth, its beauty and greatness, they have always become aware that this existence is an existence for which they owe thanks."

During this Camino, I did experience some of the poverty of human existence in the suffering and uncertainty of the journey, which caused me to turn with greater fervor to the Lord for help. Yet there were many profound joys as well — "the fullness of human existence" — especially in the people I met and in the final days of celebration in Santiago de Compostela. God was present in the wonder of these events, and for this, I will always be grateful. With the successful completion of the Camino, I can now pray the ancient prayer from the *Codex Calixtinus* with a fuller understanding of the words: "O God who has ended these feast days of your blessed apostle St. James by giving us great joy, grant to us, we humbly pray, the grace to arrive at those feasts which are not annual celebrations, but which last for all eternity." Amen.

FOUR

Conclusion

When Pope Benedict XVI was asked about his numerous trips to Spain and the resilient nature of Spain's Catholic Faith, he stated, "I would attribute that precisely to a vitality of faith that is apparently rooted in the DNA of the Spanish people."[55] That DNA came from the one who planted the Catholic seed in Spain: St. James the Apostle.

My pilgrimage to Santiago de Compostela left a deep impression upon me about the importance of St. James in the history of the Catholic Church. As an apostle, he had taken the gospel to the ends of the earth as they knew it during his time, to the Iberian Peninsula. Ever since that time, St. James has fulfilled his title of patron of Spain by continually protecting the land where his sacred relics are revered and always keeping the Iberian Peninsula within the fold of the Catholic Church.

When the Roman Empire crumbled and the Visigoths invaded Spain, the barbarians were not only converted to the

---

[55] Benedict XVI, *The Light of the World: The Pope, the Church, and the Signs of the Times* (San Francisco: Ignatius Press, 2010), 115.

Catholic Faith, but under the guidance of St. Isidore of Seville, Spain grew to be a cultural center during a time when most of Europe fell into the "Dark Ages."[56] Even while the Muslims occupied the Iberian Peninsula for seven hundred years, this chosen land never lost the Faith. In fact, Spain is the only country in history ever conquered by the Muslims that eventually regained its autonomy, showing that the Muslims may have gained power, but the heart of Spain was still faithful to Christ. Furthermore, when the Protestant Reformation divided the rest of Europe, Spain kept its Catholic Faith secure.

While no nation is perfect in this fallen world, the genius of Spain in history seems to be its ability to have created a dynamic Catholic culture for many years where large numbers of people were able to successfully achieve holiness of life. The countless number of Spanish saints gives abundant witness to this fact.

Spain and Portugal were then the chosen instruments of God to bring the Catholic Faith to the rest of the world—from Mexico to the southern tip of Argentina. While much has been written about the greed and injustices of the conquistadors of the New World, the Catholic Faith inspired by St. James was the nobler and more enduring contribution of this period of colonization. Countless missionary priests, such as the courageous Dominican friar Antonio Montesino[57] or the holy Franciscan bishop Juan de

---

[56] Thurston, *Butler's Lives of the Saints,* vol. 2, 26.
[57] Hubert Herring, *A History of Latin America From the Beginning to the Present* (New York: Alfred A. Knopf, 1965), 173–174.

Conclusion

Zumarraga,[58] fought to defend the dignity of the native peoples against the corrupt hands of the conquistadors, and this gives testimony to the fact that the Catholic Church was the voice of justice during this turbulent era. As Latin American historian Hubert Herring has written: "The man with the Cross finally proved mightier than the man with the Sword. The soldier won the battles, but the friar won the hearts. The last Spanish flag in America has long since been hauled down, but the faith of the mother country remains as the most tenacious bond among Spain's former vassals."[59]

Today, there are scores of cities throughout the Caribbean and Central and South America named after Santiago; from 1504 to 1605 alone, thirty-one cities from the Caribbean to Chile were named after Santiago.[60] Hundreds, if not thousands, of churches bear the name Santiago in these regions as well. Many have developed their own dances and foods surrounding St. James's annual feast day on July 25, which are still in use to this day. Finally, the three most populated Catholic countries in the world today—Brazil, Mexico, and the Philippines—were all evangelized through the Iberian Peninsula. Is it possible to imagine how different the world would look today if Protestant England had colonized this part of the world? How different would the world be today if the Muslims had been the first to reach the "New

---

[58] Mary Amatora, "Bishop Zumárraga: Defender of the Indians," in *A Handbook on Guadalupe*, ed. Franciscan Friars of the Immaculate (New Bedford, Massachusetts: The Academy of the Immaculate, 1997), 48; and Herring, *A History of Latin America*, 177–178.

[59] Herring, *A History of Latin America*, 169.

[60] Cardaillac, *Santiago Apóstol*, 191–192.

World" rather than Catholic Spain? Truly, St. James is a great apostle, perhaps second only to St. Paul, in evangelizing to the ends of the earth.

Lastly, I have had the honor of serving the Hispanic community for my entire priesthood. St. James was the first apostle to the Hispanics, and therefore, I believe that he still has an essential role to play for us here in the United States where the vibrant Hispanic presence has so dramatically changed the face of the Church in recent years. I pray that Santiago will intercede for the Catholic Church in the United States; that St. James would be that powerful defender who keeps us from drifting off into secularism or defective versions of the Faith, and instead would forge within us that strong bond to the one, holy, Catholic, and apostolic Faith.

Appendix

Homily at Santiago Cathedral by Pope Benedict XVI During the Jubilee Year of 2010

His Holiness, Pope Benedict XVI, visiting Santiago de Compostela in 2010

My Dear Brothers and Sisters in Jesus Christ, I give thanks to God for the gift of being here in this splendid square filled with artistic, cultural and spiritual significance. During this Holy Year, I come among you as a pilgrim among pilgrims, in the company of all those who come here thirsting for faith in the Risen Christ, a faith proclaimed and transmitted with fidelity by the apostles, among whom was James the Great, who has been venerated at Compostela from time immemorial.

I extend my gratitude to the Most Reverend Julián Barrio Barrio, Archbishop of this local church, for his words of welcome, to their Royal Highnesses, the Prince and Princess of Asturias for their kind presence, and likewise to the Cardinals and to my many Brother Bishops and priests here today. My greeting also goes to members of the Camino de Santiago group of the European Parliament, as well as to the national, regional and local authorities who are attending this celebration. This is eloquent of respect for the Successor of Peter and also of the profound emotion that Saint James of Compostela awakens in Galicia and in the other peoples of Spain, which recognizes the Apostle as its patron and protector. I also extend warm greetings to the consecrated persons, seminarians and lay faithful who take part in this Eucharistic celebration, and in a very special way I greet the pilgrims who carry on the genuine spirit of Saint James, without which little or nothing can be understood of what takes place here.

With admirable simplicity, the first reading states: "The apostles gave witness to the resurrection of the Lord with great power" (Acts 4:33). Indeed, at the beginning of all that Christianity has been and still is, we are confronted not with

Appendix

a human deed or project, but with God, who declares Jesus to be just and holy in the face of the sentence of a human tribunal that condemned Him as a blasphemer and a subversive; God who rescued Jesus from death; God who will do justice to all who have been unjustly treated in history. The apostles proclaim: "We are witnesses to these things and so is the Holy Spirit whom God gives to those who are obedient to Him" (Acts 5:32). Thus they gave witness to the life, death, and resurrection of Christ Jesus, whom they knew as He preached and worked miracles. Brothers and sisters, today we are called to follow the example of the apostles, coming to know the Lord better day by day and bearing clear and valiant witness to His Gospel. We have no greater treasure to offer to our contemporaries. In this way, we will imitate St. Paul who, in the midst of so many tribulations, setbacks, and solitude, joyfully exclaimed: "We have this treasure in earthenware vessels, to show that such transcendent power does not come from us" (2 Cor 4:7).

Beside these words of the Apostle of the Gentiles stand those of the Gospel that we have just heard; they invite us to draw life from the humility of Christ who, following in every way the will of His Father, came to serve, "to give His life in ransom for many" (Mt 20:28). For those disciples who seek to follow and imitate Christ, service of neighbor is no mere option but an essential part of their being. It is a service that is not measured by worldly standards of what is immediate, material, or apparent, but one that makes present the love of God to all in every way and bears witness to Him even in the simplest of actions. Proposing this new way of dealing with one another within the community, based on the logic of love and service, Jesus also addresses "the rulers of the nations" since, where self-giving to others is lacking, there arise forms of arrogance and exploitation that leave no room for an authentic integral human promotion. I would like this message to reach all young people: this core content of the Gospel shows you in particular the path by which, in renouncing a selfish and short-sighted way of thinking so common today, and taking on instead Jesus' own way of thinking, you may attain fulfillment and become a seed of hope.

The celebration of this Holy Year of Compostela also brings this to mind. This is what, in the secret of their heart, knowing it explicitly or sensing it without being able to express it, so many pilgrims experience as they walk the way to Santiago de Compostela to embrace the Apostle. The fatigue of the journey, the variety of landscapes, their encounter with peoples of other nationalities—all of this opens their heart to what is the deepest and most common bond that unites us as human beings: we are in quest, we need truth and beauty, we need an experience of grace, charity, peace, forgiveness, and redemption. And in the depth of each of us there resounds the presence of God and the working of the Holy Spirit. Yes, to everyone who seeks inner silence, who keeps passions, desires, and immediate occupations at a distance, to the one who prays, God grants the light to find him and to acknowledge Christ. Deep down, all those who come on pilgrimage to Santiago do so in order to encounter God who, reflected in the majesty of Christ, welcomes and blesses them as they reach the Portico de la Gloria.

Appendix

From this place, as a messenger of the Gospel sealed by the blood of Peter and James, I raise my eyes to the Europe that came in pilgrimage to Compostela. What are its great needs, fears, and hopes? What is the specific and fundamental contribution of the Church to that Europe which for half a century has been moving towards new forms and projects? Her contribution is centered on a simple and decisive reality: God exists and He has given us life. He alone is absolute, faithful, and unfailing love, that infinite goal that is glimpsed behind the good, the true, and the beautiful things of this world, admirable indeed, but insufficient for the human heart.

Saint Teresa of Jesus understood this when she wrote: "God alone suffices." Tragically, above all in nineteenth century Europe, the conviction grew that God is somehow man's antagonist and an enemy of his freedom. As a result, there was an attempt to obscure the true biblical faith in the God who sent into the world His Son Jesus Christ, so that no one should perish but that all might have eternal life (cf. Jn 3:16).

The author of the Book of Wisdom, faced with a paganism in which God envied or despised humans, puts it clearly: how could God have created all things if He did not love them, He who in his infinite fullness, has need of nothing (cf. Wis 11:24–26)? Why would He have revealed Himself to human beings if He did not wish to take care of them? God is the origin of our being and the foundation and apex of our freedom, not its opponent. How can mortal man build a firm foundation and how can the sinner be reconciled with himself? How can it be that there is public silence with regard to the first and essential reality of human life? How can what is most decisive in life be confined to the purely private sphere or banished to the shadows? We cannot live in darkness, without seeing the light of the sun. How is it then that God, Who is the light of every mind, the power of every will, and the magnet of every heart, be denied the right to propose the light that dissipates all darkness? This is why we need to hear God once again under the skies of Europe; may this holy word not be spoken in vain, and may it not be put at the service of purposes other than its own. It needs to be spoken in a holy way. And we must hear it in this way in ordinary life, in the silence of work, in brotherly love, and in the difficulties that years bring on.

Europe must open itself to God, must come to meet Him without fear, and work with His grace for that human dignity which was discerned by her best traditions: not only the biblical, at the basis of this order, but also the classical, the medieval and the modern, the matrix from which the great philosophical, literary, cultural, and social masterpieces of Europe were born.

This God and this man were concretely and historically manifested in Christ. It is this Christ whom we can find all along the way to Compostela for, at every juncture, there is a cross which welcomes and points the way. The cross, which is the supreme sign of love brought to its extreme and hence both gift and pardon, must be our guiding star in the night of time. The Cross and love, the Cross and light have been

Appendix

synonymous in our history because Christ allowed Himself to hang there in order to give us the supreme witness of His love, to invite us to forgiveness and reconciliation, to teach us how to overcome evil with good. So do not fail to learn the lessons of that Christ whom we encounter at the crossroads of our journey and our whole life, in whom God comes forth to meet us as our friend, father, and guide. Blessed Cross, shine always upon the lands of Europe!

Allow me here to point out the glory of man, and to indicate the threats to his dignity resulting from the privation of his essential values and richness, and the marginalization and death visited upon the weakest and the poorest. One cannot worship God without taking care of his sons and daughters; and man cannot be served without asking who his Father is and answering the question about Him. The Europe of science and technology, the Europe of civilization and culture, must be at the same time a Europe open to transcendence and fraternity with other continents, and open to the living and true God, starting with the living and true man.

This is what the Church wishes to contribute to Europe: to be watchful for God and for man, based on the understanding of both which is offered to us in Jesus Christ.

Dear friends, let us raise our eyes in hope to all that God has promised and offers us. May He give us His strength; may He reinvigorate the Archdiocese of Santiago de Compostela; may He renew the faith of His sons and daughters and assist them in fidelity to their vocation to sow and strengthen the Gospel, at home and abroad.

May Saint James, the companion of the Lord, obtain abundant blessings for Galicia and the other peoples of Spain, elsewhere in Europe and overseas, wherever the Apostle is a sign of Christian identity and a promoter of the proclamation of Christ.

About the Author

Fr. Greg J. Markey was ordained a priest for the Diocese of Bridgeport in 1999 and currently serves as Head Chaplain at Thomas Aquinas College in Northfield, Massachusetts.

Sophia Institute

Sophia Institute is a nonprofit institution that seeks to nurture the spiritual, moral, and cultural life of souls and to spread the gospel of Christ in conformity with the authentic teachings of the Roman Catholic Church.

Sophia Institute Press fulfills this mission by offering translations, reprints, and new publications that afford readers a rich source of the enduring wisdom of mankind.

Sophia Institute also operates the popular online resource CatholicExchange.com. *Catholic Exchange* provides world news from a Catholic perspective as well as daily devotionals and articles that will help readers to grow in holiness and live a life consistent with the teachings of the Church.

In 2013, Sophia Institute launched Sophia Institute for Teachers to renew and rebuild Catholic culture through service to Catholic education. With the goal of nurturing the spiritual, moral, and cultural life of souls, and an abiding respect for the role and work of teachers, we strive to provide materials and programs that are at once enlightening to the mind and ennobling to the heart; faithful and complete, as well as useful and practical.

Sophia Institute gratefully recognizes the Solidarity Association for preserving and encouraging the growth of our apostolate over the course of many years. Without their generous and timely support, this book would not be in your hands.

www.SophiaInstitute.com
www.CatholicExchange.com
www.SophiaInstituteforTeachers.org

Sophia Institute Press is a registered trademark of Sophia Institute.
Sophia Institute is a tax-exempt institution as defined by the Internal Revenue Code, Section 501(c)(3). Tax ID 22-2548708.